A collector's history of English Pottery

Griselda Lewis is an enthusiastic collector of English pottery whose fresh approach to the subject has led her into fields that are still inadequately charted. Pratt ware is an example: the first results of her researches into the varied origins of this delightful, brightly coloured ware appeared recently in *Antiques* magazine. But her interests in English pottery – 'this lovable subject' as she calls it – is not limited to one particular potter or type of pottery. Her knowledge and enthusiasm for everything from bronze age beakers to the work of such modern potters as Hans Coper is remarkable; they constitute one of the many charms of this book.

A collector's history of
English Pottery

Griselda Lewis

A Studio Book

THE VIKING PRESS New York

Title-page illustration
Unglazed earthenware intaglio mould, made by the firm of Wood and Caldwell (Enoch Wood)
anytime from 1790–1818. Impressed mark on the back. Same size as original.

© Griselda Lewis, 1969
Designed by Gillian Greenwood
All rights reserved
Published in the United States, 1969 by The Viking Press, Inc.
625, Madison Avenue, New York, N.Y. 10022
Library of Congress Catalog Card Number: 78-80264
Published in Great Britain 1969 by Studio Vista Ltd
Blue Star House, Highgate Hill, London N19
Set in 11 pt Plantin, 1 point leaded
Printed in the Netherlands by Drukkerij Reclame NV, Rotterdam
Bound in Great Britain

SBN 970 22921 0

Contents

Acknowledgements

My thanks are especially due to the following people who have helped me in so many ways over the new edition of the book.

Mr Robert Allbrook, Allied English Potteries, Mr Weightman, Miss Linscott and Mr A. Shelley; Mr Michael Archer of the Victoria and Albert Museum, Mr Tom Arnold, Mrs Natalie Bevan, Mr P. D. C. Brown of the Ashmolean Museum, Mr R. J. Charleston, Keeper: Ceramic Department of the Victoria and Albert Museum, Mr David T–D Clarke of the Colchester and Essex Museum, Mr Norman Cook of the Guildhall Museum, the Council of Industrial Design, Mr Euan Cooper-Willis, the Countess of Cranbrook, Sir Arthur Elton, Mr J. S. Goddard, Mr Hugh Green, Mr Geoffrey A. Godden, Professor Guyatt of the Royal College of Art, Mr John Hadfield, Mr John Hall, Mr Roy Holland, Mr Robert Jefferson, Mrs Elizabeth Jenkins, Mr E. J. Laws of the City Museum, Nottingham, Miss Agnes Lothian, Miss F. Lovering, D. M. & P. Manheim Ltd, Mr Nicholas Meinertzhagen, Mr Arnold Mountford of the City Museum and Art Gallery Stoke on Trent, Mr Peter O'Malley, Miss Elizabeth Owles of the Ipswich Museum, Mr and Mrs David Pearce, Mr and Mrs Jasper A. Peck, The Pharmaceutical Society, Dr Martin Pritchard, Professor Queensberry of the Royal College of Art, Mr Hugh Radcliffe-Wilson, Royal Doulton Potteries, Sotheby and Co, Wedgwood and Co Ltd, particularly Mr Derek Halfpenny and Miss Judith Turner, Dr John F. Wilkinson, Mr H. Francis Wood and all the artist potters who have so kindly provided me with photographs of their work and also to Mr Bob Alcock and Mr John Webb for all the trouble they have taken in producing so many good photographs.

GRISELDA LEWIS

AUTHOR'S NOTE

Some of the material in this book originally appeared in my earlier publication, A Picture History of English Pottery (1956). The text of the Collector's History of English Pottery has been completely rewritten and a great deal of new material has been incorporated, both in the text and in the photographic section.

1 Early pottery in England

Because of its enduring quality, pottery-making is the oldest surviving craft practised by man—except for the making of weapons. The basic necessity for survival was food; omniverous man made spears and arrows in order to kill animals to eat, and when tired of eating them raw, made primitive pots in which to cook them, to store his food and to drink from. So, where clay was to be found, pots could be made. They were probably first made by the women as part of the household chores, while the men did the hunting.

The earliest English pottery to survive belongs to the first Neolithic period or New Stone Age (c. 3000–2000 BC). Though pieces are seldom found in anything but a fragmentary state, it has been possible for skilled archaeologists to restore them sufficiently for us to see what they were like. And they were just about as primitive as it was possible to be, for the earliest pots are small round-bottomed bowls made of very coarse clay, dark in colour, shaped by hand and hardened by burning on an open fire. This kind of pottery has been found in East Anglia and in the hill forts of southern England. Sometimes the shapes were a little less basic, for the rims were sometimes rolled or beaded and occasionally handles occur in the form of loops or lugs.

Some slightly later pottery dating from about 2000 BC is of quite a different shape, being quite flat-bottomed and in the form of a shallow bucket or plant-pot. These are thought to have been this shape because the people who made them probably used wooden vessels before, and this is the shape those wooden vessels could have been.

The pottery that survives from the Bronze Age (c. 1900–450 BC) is often in a well-preserved state, for it was buried deliberately with the ashes of the dead. The Bronze Age cinerary urns made to hold these cremated remains probably did not differ very much from the household cooking and storage pots of the time. The beakers and urns of this period, though shaped by hand, were well-formed and decorated with incised patterns of herring-bone or cross-hatched bands, made with a pointed stick; or sometimes with lines made by the impressing of a thong or cord in the damp clay, or patterns made with a finger nail.

The potter's wheel was introduced into this country during the last phase of the Early Iron Age (somewhere about 75 BC) and, dating from this period, are well-thrown, though rather clumsy shapes, ornamented with wheel-turned decorations.

When the Romans first came to Britain, they imported a quantity of red-gloss pottery from Gaul, Italy and the Rhineland, but by the second century AD, Roman potters, (no doubt aided by the native British) were at work in England and the red-gloss ware was certainly produced at Colchester in Essex, where some pieces of moulds and some hundreds of fragments have been found. It was of a much poorer quality than that made on the continent.

At about the beginning of the second century AD a distinctive type of pottery was made at Castor, near Peterborough in Northamptonshire. Some of this was a light-bodied earthenware of varying hardness, and a dark purplish red colour; it was often decorated with slip of the same colour trailed on the surface like cake icing, in abstract scroll patterns or animal forms. But the most attractive ware made at Castor had a smooth black body and was decorated with white slip. Judging by contemporary standards, it was surprisingly thin and delicately potted. Castor ware was made until the late fourth or early fifth century AD. At the same time, pottery of a similar type was made in other places, notably in the New Forest; but useful ware of all kinds including storage jars, cooking pots, mortars for grinding corn, feeding bottles and burial urns must have been made in considerable quantities wherever potteries existed, for a large amount of Romano-British pottery survives. Twenty-five kilns were found in Colchester alone.

After the retreat of the Romans from these islands in the early fifth century, a period of disorder and lawlessness prevailed. The British seem to have spent all their energies on keeping alive and defending their families and property from a series of foreign invaders. What pottery survives from this time is of a strictly utilitarian nature and coarsely made. The influence of the Roman potters declined, the use of the potters' wheel lapsed and the Anglo-Saxons shaped all their pottery by hand. They had almost reverted to the standards of the Stone Age. They lived in a very primitive way in wooden buildings, of which only traces of post holes in the ground remain.

The pagan Saxons, living in south-eastern England, cremated their dead and put the ashes of the bones into urns which they made for the purpose. Though hand-shaped, sometimes these urns were decorated with quite complicated patterns made by the use of stamps (which they carved from bones) and incised lines. Sometimes the decoration was in the form of raised 'blisters', either pushed up from the interior of the pot, or else applied on top as an extra layer, though this type of decoration was more usual on the continent.

In the late sixth century, there is the first evidence (since the Roman occupation) of a professional potter at work, who must have traded his wares. This potter's work has been found at Lackford, not far from Thetford, and his pots have also been found at Icklingham, West Stow Heath and as far away as Cambridge. The ware can be identified by the similarity of basic material, of shape and by his very characteristic use of decoration, consisting of horizontal bands of incised lines and pendant triangles of small stamped marks (rather like bunches of grapes) outlined by more incised lines. (See page 15).

By the mid-seventh century the wheel was back in use again. In East Anglia some kilns were in production at Ipswich, and later a wheel was being used again at Thetford, where a pottery was established for the making of ware similar to that found at Ipswich. This was in about 850 and the production continued into the twelfth century. This Thetford ware (so-called because the kilns at Thetford happened to be discovered first) is grey in colour and has very marked grooves round the outside made by the tips of the fingers of the potter. The shapes are

1

2

3

4

1 Small almost black irregularly shaped cooking pot. New Stone Age *c.* 3000–2000 BC.
An example of the earliest and most primitive pottery found in England. Found at Dales Road brickfields, Ipswich. Height 3″. *Ipswich Museum*

2 Flat bottomed shallow plant-pot shaped bowl with incised decoration dating from *c.* 2000 BC.
The clay is reddish brown in colour and the shape is inspired by that of a wooden vessel. Found at Creeting St Mary, Suffolk. Height 4½″. *Ipswich Museum*

3 Early Bronze Age beaker with incised decoration *c.* 1900–1400 BC. Found at Goodmanham, East Riding, Yorkshire. Height 6¾″. *Victoria & Albert Museum*

4 Middle Bronze Age burial urn with overhanging rim and incised bands of decoration. *c.* 1400–1000 BC. Found at Kempston, Bedfordshire. Height 8″. *Victoria & Albert Museum*

simple with relatively thin walls; urns, jars, jugs or pitchers with slightly turned over rims were made, not so very different in character from the coarser pottery made at the time of the Roman occupation.

The pottery at Ipswich must have had quite high standards, for a good many slightly deformed but usable pieces had been discarded as wasters. Among these were some pieces fired to a brownish red instead of the characteristic ashy grey. The wrong colour was enough to class them as seconds.

Although it is unlikely that any early pottery will turn up in a sale-room or a shop, it is not at all unlikely that discoveries of buried pottery, even if fragmentary, will still be made. Important finds have recently been made during the clearing of building sites. The deeper than usual ploughing of farm land can unearth a Roman or Saxon cemetery, and even the process of digging a garden or the clearing of a moat can be rewarded by the finding of pieces of pottery from which we can learn something of our predecessors.

The domestic pottery of mediaeval England was much less refined than that produced at the time of the Roman occupation. The most usual pottery vessels were jugs or pitchers, for at this time the ordinary people ate off wooden platters and drank from vessels made of horn or wood, whereas the nobility and the rich merchants used metal plates, jugs and cups. Pottery was mostly confined to the kitchen or the peasant's hut. Even so, the pieces that have been preserved to this day can hardly be dismissed as uninteresting. They may be crude, but they are remarkable for their bold shapes and the diversity of their decoration. The jugs and pitchers of the thirteenth century were rather tall and attenuated, whereas those of the later fourteenth or fifteenth centuries became broader in the base and less high. Some of the ware was left unglazed and undecorated, but much was patterned with a different coloured slip, or with incised lines, or decorated with reliefs stamped in different coloured clays, which were made with a wooden stamp cut in intaglio. The only known glaze at that time had a lead basis and developed a yellowish colour in the firing. Sometimes the glaze was stained with copper, giving it a variety of greens and some of the later ware was stained with manganese and oxide of iron, which produced various rich browns. The glaze was sprinkled or dusted on to the surface with a rag. Sometimes it was confined to only a part of a vessel; many mediaeval jugs have only a bib of glaze under the spout. Owing to the primitive methods of firing pottery, impurities were always present in the kilns and this accounts for the generally dark appearance of the ware. In addition to domestic pottery, tiles were made for the decoration of churches and abbeys. The designs on these tiles were either incised or impressed, modelled in low relief or inlaid, or occasionally decorated with slip. They were often glazed.

Much of the ware of Tudor times, though rather coarse, was glazed either with a plain lead glaze giving a yellow effect, or else with a green-stained lead glaze. The objects that have been found range from candle-sticks to chamber-pots and include costrels or pilgrims' bottles.

During the first half of the sixteenth century, that is up to 1540 when Henry VIII ordered the dissolution of the monasteries, a particularly good ware was much used by the monks. This has been given somewhat loosely the name of 'Cister-

5

6

7

8

5 Early Iron Age (third period) pedestal urn. *c.* 75 BC. This has been thrown on a wheel. From the cremation cemetery at Aylesford, Kent. Height 9¾″. *Victoria & Albert Museum*

6 Early Iron Age butt beaker. *c.* 75 BC. Wheel thrown and with wheel turned and rouletted decoration. Found at Sutton Courtney, Berks. Height 6¾″. *Victoria & Albert Museum*

7 Known as The Colchester Vase. *c.* AD 200. The decoration shows a combat between two gladiators Memnon and Valentinus. It is not absolutely certain whether this was made in Colchester, but similar ware was made there. Height 8½″. *Colchester and Essex Museum*

8 Castor ware vase or beaker, black with white slip decoration. *c.* AD 400. Found in Broad Street, London. Height 5⅝″. *Guildhall Museum*

cian' ware, merely because so many pieces were found in the ruins of the Cistercian Abbeys in Yorkshire, though pieces of similar pottery have been found all over the country as far apart as Ely and Abergavenny. This ware is quite smooth and thin, made of red clay and glazed with a dark brown or almost black glaze.

A similar ware was made in Burslem from the beginning of the seventeenth century for about a hundred years. This was glazed with the usual lead glaze with the addition of crude oxide of iron and though always very dark in colour, the tone varies, as does the brilliance of the glaze due to the degree of reduction during firing and the amount of iron in the glaze. This ware was made in other places in Staffordshire and in Shropshire during the nineteenth century.

Drinking vessels with one or more handles known as tygs are typical of this ware. They were probably used in some public houses during the eighteenth century, for there is one in the City Museum at Stoke-on-Trent with the excise mark of Queen Anne upon it.

It is difficult to present the history of English pottery in an orderly chronological pattern. Until the middle of the sixteenth century developments were slow, and then tin-glazing was introduced. Towards the end of the seventeenth century the production of stoneware began. Throughout the eighteenth century one improvement or invention followed another with almost bewildering rapidity, it was the great age of change and growth in the pottery industry. But because a new technique was introduced, it did not mean that old ways were superseded at once; tradition dies hard, and thus we have an overlapping of techniques that is sometimes extremely confusing.

9 Romano-British burial urns dating from the second century AD, from the Roman cemeteries at Colchester. Height: average 9″–10″. *Colchester and Essex Museum*

10 Pagan Saxon burial urn. Hand-shaped and decorated with stamps and incised lines. Late 6th century AD. Urns very similar in every way to this one have been found at West Stow Heath, Icklingham and near Cambridge. All obviously made by the same hand, known as the 'Lackford Potter'. Found at Lackford. Height 9″. *Ashmolean Museum, Oxford*

11 'Thetford' ware storage jar. 7th–9th century. Although the potters' wheel was in use again, the pottery at this time was more primitive than that made in the second century AD. Height 8″. *Ipswich Museum*

9

10

11

15

12

meam: auribus perm

14

13

15   16   17

12 Lead-glazed red tiles inlaid with white clay, from Chertsey Abbey. *c.* 1275. The architecture of the canopies above the Queen, Bishop and King is in the style of the late thirteenth century. Height 31″. *British Museum*

13 The circular tile from Chertsey Abbey is of a slightly earlier date. It shows King Richard in single combat with the Sultan Saladin at Babylon. 16″ square. *British Museum*

14 Decoration taken from the Luttrell Psalter. *c.* 1340. *British Museum*

15 Baluster jug, with traces of a yellowish lead glaze. *c.* 1275. Found in Blossoms Inn yard, Lawrence Lane, London. Height 18″. *Guildhall Museum*

16 Jug decorated with incised and rouletted patterns and covered with a yellowish green lead glaze. *c.* 1300. Found at Scarborough. Height 14⅝″. *Fitzwilliam Museum*

17 Rope-handled jug, elaborately decorated with knights in armour in high relief round the neck, and stags attacked by hounds round the body. *c.* 1275–1325. Made of buff coloured clay, glazed with a dark apple green lead glaze. Found in Friars Lane, Nottingham. Height 14″. *Nottingham Museum*

18 19 20

21 22

23

24
25

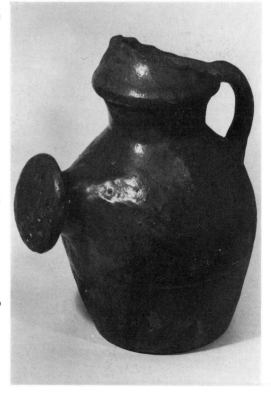

18 Buff earthenware pitcher with a bearded face each side and a brownish yellow glaze merging to light apple green, three quarters of the way down. The vertical stripes are purplish black. Found on a kiln site in Nottingham. *c.* 1300. Height 20″. *Nottingham Museum*

19 Very beautiful red earthenware jug with trailed white slip decoration under a yellow lead glaze. *c.* 1300. Found at Austin Friars, London. Height 14¾″. *Guildhall Museum*

20 Buff earthenware jug with a bearded face, a fore-runner of the Toby jug; the decoration is green and brown under a yellow lead glaze. *c.* 1350. Found in Bishopsgate Street, London. Height 11″. *Guildhall Museum*

21 Dark buff coloured jug with a face, covered with a mottled green glaze. *c.* 1350. Height 11¼″. *Fitzwilliam Museum*

22 Red earthenware pitcher with white slip applied decoration and a lead glaze. *c.* 1350. Height 8¾″. *Fitzwilliam Museum*

23 Puzzle jug of light red earthenware with a coating of white slip, covered with a dark green glaze. The date, 1571 is made of applied strips of clay. Height 11¼″. *Fitzwilliam Museum*

24 Late fifteenth-century watering pot of dark red-brown earthenware decorated with white slip. It was filled by submersion; a thumb was then put over the hole in the top and the pot swung, base upwards. The watering was then done by swinging the pot back and forth, when the water sprinkled out through the holes in the base. Height 11¼″. *Guildhall Museum*

25 Watering pot of dark red earthenware partly glazed with a lead glaze. *c.* 1550. Height 10½″. *Brighton Museum*

26

26 Candle bracket of pale buff coloured clay covered with a yellow lead glaze. *c.* 1575. The moulded design shows the arms of Elizabeth I and a Tudor rose with the royal cypher. Height 17½″. *British Museum*

27   28

29

27 Costrel or pilgrim's bottle of buff coloured clay glazed with a green glaze. *c.* 1509–47. Height 6″. *British Museum*

28 Two-handled tyg. *c.* 1660. Made in Staffordshire and glazed with a dark shiny iron glaze. Similar to the ware found in the ruins of the Yorkshire monastries and called loosely 'Cistercian' ware. Height 6½″. *City Museum, Stoke-on-Trent*

29 Many handled tyg. *c.* 1660. Made in Staffordshire. Height 5¼″. *City Museum, Stoke-on-Trent*

30 Large circular dish, decorated with a pattern of inn signs. The white slip has been cut away to make the design, exposing the light red of the clay beneath. Glazed with a yellowish lead glaze, slightly mottled with green. Made by John Livermore at the Wrotham pottery in 1647. Dia. 17⅜″. *Fitzwilliam Museum*

22

2 Slipware

LEAD-GLAZED SLIP-DECORATED EARTHENWARE OF THE
SEVENTEENTH AND EIGHTEENTH CENTURIES

Slip is clay mixed with water to the consistency of cream. It can be used in various ways to decorate pottery. Slip of one colour can be applied in a thin all-over coating to the clay body of another colour either by brushing or immersion, and a design can then be trailed on to the surface through a narrow tube (originally a quill) using slips of different colours, or the slip can be applied in lines or stripes, then combed to make a marbled or feathered effect. Or the design can be scratched through the top layer of slip to expose the body of a different colour beneath (*sgraffito*) or the slip can be inlaid (in the same way as the mediaeval tiles).

Although slip decoration was used by the Romans and also in mediaeval times, this method of decoration was not fully exploited until the seventeenth century. Slipware was made throughout the eighteenth century and was still made by various country potters in the nineteenth century. The traditional methods of slip decoration have been used to the present day by many studio potters, with varying degrees of success.

Slipware was made in many places, but principally at Wrotham in Kent and in Staffordshire. Most of the slipware found in and around London and loosely termed 'Metropolitan' is now known to have been made at Harlow in Essex.

Slipware of a very characteristic kind was made in Devonshire, at potteries at Bideford, Fremington and Barnstaple (from about 1600), and inlaid slip decoration was used at Rye and Chailey in Sussex in the late eighteenth and early nineteenth century. Other centres where slipware was made include Gestingthorpe and Castle Hedingham in Essex (in the nineteenth century); Tickenhall in Derbyshire and Bolsover near Chesterfield; in Buckinghamshire, Cambridgeshire, and at Fareham and Fordingbridge in Hampshire; High Halden in Kent; in Nottingham; in Somerset at Donyatt and Pill near Bristol; Polesworth in Warwickshire and in Wiltshire near Salisbury; in Yorkshire at Midhope, Burton-in-Lonsdale and Halifax as well as near Wakefield. Also at Bridgend and Ewenny in Glamorganshire.

The known history of the pottery at Wrotham dates from the beginning of the seventeenth century, the earliest dated piece known to have come from here being dated 1612. Production continued well into the eighteenth century. John Livermore, who died in 1658 (and who made the dish illustrated on page 22) was working here and also Henry Ifield (who died in 1673) and George Richardson (who died 1687) and who was known to have marked the ware with the word 'Wrotham'. A characteristic of the decoration from this pottery was the use of 'sprigged' designs. That is, the application of a design stamped out in a different coloured clay. Most of the known pieces from Wrotham are tygs and jugs.

Without doubt the most spectacular pieces of slipware were made in Staffordshire during the last thirty years of the seventeenth century and the first decade of the eighteenth. These were large circular dishes or chargers some 16 inches to 22 inches in diameter and made by Thomas Toft and his son of the same name, Ralph Toft, and James Toft (the brother of Thomas the younger); John and William Wright, George Taylor, William Talor and Ralph Simpson. Most of these large dishes were decorated in a similar manner with a trellis border with a name or inscription, and an elaborately drawn design of trailed and dotted slip, on a coating of white slip in black, brown, orange or white. The whole under a yellow lead glaze.

The illustrated subjects include the Royal Arms with the lion and unicorn, King Charles II hiding in an oak, or accompanied by his wife Catherine of Braganza, or a Bishop; William III and George I, cavaliers and heraldic designs. Apart from these large and handsome dishes, which were obviously made more for decoration than use, many other slip-decorated pieces were made in Staffordshire including tygs and teapots, cradles and baking-dishes.

The so-called 'Metropolitan' slipware has always been something of a puzzle, because although quantities of tygs and other pieces had been found in London, no kiln site with sherds and wasters had ever come to light. This Metropolitan ware was made of a light brown clay which fired to quite a bright red, or to a darker brownish red. Unlike much of the Staffordshire slipware, the ware was not first coated with white slip, but the pattern was trailed directly on to the body of the piece. The patterns were not very imaginative, consisting of rather crudely drawn zigzags or herringbone designs and many are inscribed with pious mottos or exhortations.

Only recently, when the site was being cleared for the building of the new town at Harlow in Essex some twenty-six miles from London, five kiln sites were discovered with literally tons of sherds, many of them with religious inscriptions and with similar designs to those on the Metropolitan ware. These kilns were discovered in the neighbourhood of Potter Street (which had been called Potter Street since the early fifteenth century).

Early in the seventeenth century a new road was built from London to Newmarket, by way of Harlow and Epping and this must have presented a very convenient way of transport for the products of the potteries that were established in this area, and which flourished throughout the seventeenth century. The shortage of specimens with dates before 1666 is no doubt due to the wholesale destruction of the Great Fire in that year.

The chief productions of these potteries were flat plates from about six to fifteen inches in diameter and rather crude tygs and jugs. They do not compare favourably either in technique or in originality of design with the work of the Staffordshire potters.

The *sgraffito* type of decoration was largely practised at the Devon potteries of Bideford, Fremington and Barnstaple, which date from the beginning of the seventeenth century. Here many large and elaborate 'Harvest' jugs were made, as well as dishes. The jugs often bear a date and sometimes a poem or an inscription. The designs included ships in full sail, the royal arms and bold floral

31

32

33

34

31 A trailed slip-decorated jug of the 'Metropolitan' type, now thought to have been made at Harlow in Essex. It bears the pious inscription 'FAST AND PRAY AND PRAY | AND PITTY THE POOR AMEND THY | LIFE AND SENNE NO MOR 1656. Height 11″. *Guildhall Museum*

32 Two-handled tyg of the 'Metropolitan' type; now thought to have been made at Harlow throughout the seventeenth century. Decorated with trailed slip. Height 7¾″. *Guildhall Museum*

33 Tyg. The red body is decorated with moulded applied ornaments made of white clay, as well as trailed slip. Made at Wrotham and dated 1695. Height 7″. *Fitzwilliam Museum*

34 Two-handled posset pot of buff coloured clay with feathered slip decoration in dark red. Round the top is the name Thomas Heath and the date 1698. Covered with a yellow lead glaze. Made in Staffordshire. Height 4¾″. *Fitzwilliam Museum*

35   Slip-decorated dish showing Charles II hiding in the Boscobel Oak. Made by William Talor in Staffordshire. *c.* 1660. Dia. 17½″. *Fitzwilliam Museum*

36   Slip-decorated Coronation Dish, showing Charles II and Archbishop William Juxon. Made by George Taylor in Staffordshire. *c.* 1661. Dia. 17¾″. *Fitzwilliam Museum*

37   Slip-decorated dish. The design shows a mermaid with a large comb and a looking-glass. Made by Ralph Toft in Staffordshire. *c.* 1670. Dia. 17¼″. *Fitzwilliam Museum*

38   Slip-decorated dish. King William III. Made by Ralph Simpson in Staffordshire. *c.* 1689. Dia. 18″. *Victoria and Albert Museum*

39 Slip-decorated dish. King George I. Made by Ralph Simpson. *c.* 1714. Dia. 17¼″. *Victoria and Albert Museum*

patterns. From Devon, much of this pottery was exported to America, the ships returning with cargoes of tobacco; this trade lasted until the middle of the eight-eenth century, when the Dutch put the Devon exporters out of business, by exporting large quantities of their Delft ware to America.

40 Slip-decorated dish. The Pelican in her Piety, made by Ralph Simpson in Staffordshire. *c.* 1714. (The border of roundels and faces is very similar to the George I dish.) Dia. 17″. *Victoria and Albert Museum*

41

42

43

41 Slip-decorated cradle. These were often dated and were made for presentation pieces to newly married couples. Dates are recorded from 1693–1839. Made in Staffordshire. *c.* 1700. Length 10″. *Victoria and Albert Museum*

42 Tyg decorated with trailed slip and bands of feathering. Made in Staffordshire. *c.* 1700. Height 4⅛″. *Victoria and Albert Museum*

43 Tyg of buff coloured earthenware with brown trailed slip dotted with white and bands of combed slip. Made in Staffordshire 1701. Height 4¼″. *Victoria and Albert Museum*

29

44 Circular earthenware dish with notched edges, decorated with marbled or joggled slip. Made in Staffordshire in the late seventeenth or early eighteenth century. Dia. 13¾″. *Victoria and Albert Museum*

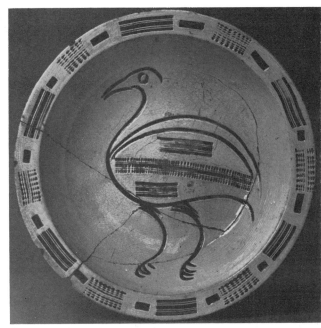

45　　　　　　　　　　　　　　　　46

47　　　　　　　　　　　　　　　　48

45　Slip-decorated owl dish. Made in Staffordshire. *c.* 1720. Dia. 16¾″. There is a similar dish in existence decorated with a hen and chickens. *City Museum, Stoke-on-Trent*

46　Circular earthenware dish. The body is an agate ware of red and buff clay coated with white slip, the design cut through it (*sgraffito*), under a straw coloured lead glaze. Made in Staffordshire in the mid-eighteenth century. Dia. 12¾″. *Fitzwilliam Museum*

47　Teapot of buff coloured earthenware with slip decoration in dark and light reds and white. Made in Staffordshire in the early eighteenth century. Height 8½″. *Fitzwilliam Museum*

48　Circular earthenware bowl, with white slip on a red body, *sgraffito* decoration. Made in Staffordshire 1755. Width 9¾″. *Victoria and Albert Museum*

31

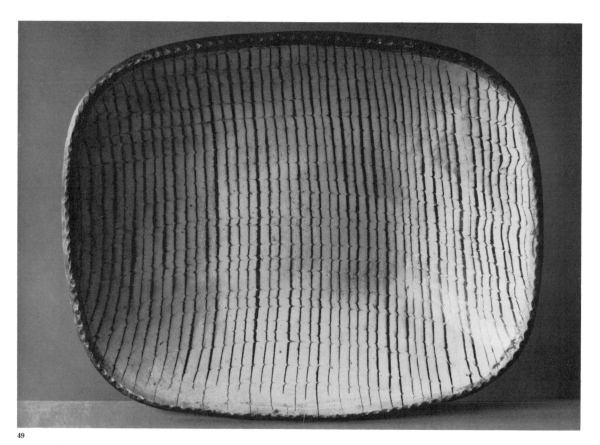

49

50

49 Baking-dish with notched edge
decorated with combed slip.
Made in Staffordshire in the
eighteenth century. 20½″ long.
Victoria and Albert Museum

50 Slipware dish with a light red
body covered with white slip
decorated with a *sgraffito*
design. There is a curious
cup-like protruberance in the
centre, not deep enough for a
candlestick. Marked with the
initials H. F. and the date
1725. Made at Bideford,
Devon. Dia. 14⅝″.

51

52

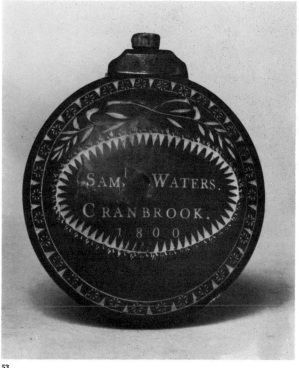

53

51 Puzzle jug with *sgraffito* decoration. Dark
red body with white slip and *sgraffito*
decoration. Round the neck is inscribed 'I B
1793'. Made at Ilminster in Somerset.
Height 8¼″. *Willett Collection, Brighton*

52 Harvest pitcher with *sgraffito* decoration.
The royal motto reads 'Hone soet que mal y
pense.' The other side is the inscription
'Harvis is com all bissey
Now Mackin your
Barley mow when me do
Laber hard and swet good
Ale is better far than meet
Bideford April 28 1775 M–W'.
Round the base are the words 'Deu et mon
drots 1775'. Height 13½″. *Royal Albert
Memorial Museum, Exeter*

53 Spirit flask. Made of red clay with incised
and impressed decoration partly made up of
printers' flowers, inlaid with a white clay and
glazed with a yellow lead glaze. On the
obverse, within a border is the verse:
'Wine cheers the heart
and warms the blood
and at this season's migh
ty good.'
Beneath are crossed branches and along the
edge the words 'SOUTH CHAILEY
POTTREY'. Height 4⅞″. Made in Sussex,
1800. *Fitzwilliam Museum*

54

55

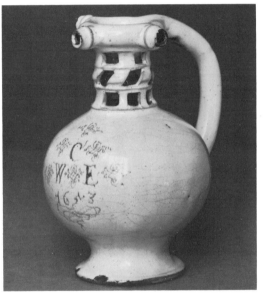

56

57

54 Jug of the Malling type, covered in a rich slightly speckled blue tin glaze. Probably made in London during the last quarter of the sixteenth century. Height 6″. *Guildhall Museum*

55 Mug painted in blue on a white ground. Round the neck are the names JOHN POTTEN & SUSANNA 1633. Made in Lambeth. Height 5⅜″. *Fitzwilliam Museum*

56 Puzzle jug, painted in blue on a white ground. Inscribed

$$\begin{array}{c} C \\ W \quad E \\ 1653 \end{array}$$

It was the custom to put the initial of the surname first, followed by the Christian name initials of the couple to whom the piece was inscribed. Made in Lambeth. Height 6⅝″. *Fitzwilliam Museum*

57 Wine jug, painted in blue, orange and yellow. Made in Lambeth 1660. Height 7″. *Fitzwilliam Museum*

3 Delft ware

We shall now have to go back a little in time to the last decades of the sixteenth century, to see quite another type of English pottery. This was of foreign origin and had nothing to do with our traditional lead-glazed slip-decorated earthenwares.

Tin-enamelled earthenware or delft, as it is usually called, is an earthenware covered with an opaque whitish glaze made from oxide of tin. It was made in Syria, Asia Minor and Egypt as early as the sixth century AD. It was first made in Europe by the Moors in Spain, then by the Italians. This technique finally arrived in England by way of the Netherlands in the middle of the sixteenth century. The main centres of production in this country were London, Bristol and Liverpool, though it was also made in Ireland and Scotland.

Though the Dutch learned their tin-glazing technique from the Italians, their actual manner of decoration was much more frequently derived from oriental porcelain, which was then being imported by the Dutch East India Company, than from the decorations on Italian maiolica. Chinese porcelain was being imported into England by the mid-seventeenth century, but it was extremely expensive and only within reach of the few. The delft ware of the English potters of this period was an attempt to provide the middle classes, who could not afford Chinese porcelain, with the best imitation they were able to make, for although delft ware was often thick and clumsy and always completely opaque, it certainly bore a superficial resemblance to Chinese porcelain. The English manufacturers of delft ware never perhaps achieved the high degree of artistic perfection reached by the Dutch, but they added something to the foreign designs which prevented them from being mere slavish copies.

There seems little doubt that London was the first place in England where delft ware was made. The earliest pieces that have been found were jugs with mottled brown or blue glaze and similar in shape to the German stoneware that was being imported into this country at that time. These early jugs are mounted in silver, which was hallmarked, so the pieces can easily be dated, some as early as 1570. One such jug (1581–2) came from the church at West Malling in Kent and two others have been found in that neighbourhood. No traces of a kiln however, have been found, and in all probability the 'Malling' jugs (as they have come to be called) were made in London.

In 1571, two Flemish potters called Jacob Janson and Jasper Andries sent a petition to Queen Elizabeth, asking for permission to settle by the banks of the Thames. They are said to have produced delft ware at a pottery near Aldgate, where they probably produced apothecaries' jars among other things, though the earliest recorded date on one of these is 1628.

A delft ware pottery was started in Southwark about 1625 and from there some craftsmen travelled to the west country and settled outside Bristol, where the Brislington pottery was founded about 1650. Other potteries making tin-glazed earthenware soon grew up in the same neighbourhood. And in London, the Lambeth pottery must have been working by the 1630's. This factory became the largest centre for the production of delft ware and continued working until the end of the eighteenth century. Typical Lambeth productions were wine bottles, pill slabs and drug jars, plates and large shallow bowls or chargers decorated with blue brush marks round the rim, and designs of formalized fruit and flowers, also scenes of the Fall and portraits of sovereigns. Arms of Liveried Companies are also found on winecups and dishes. Many other objects were also made including fuddling cups, puzzle jugs, mugs, candlesticks, barbers' dishes, bleeding bowls, posset pots and vases and even ornaments and tiles. The choice of decoration was very varied and often the only colour to be used was blue, derived from cobalt. Sometimes this would be combined with a decoration in white on a very pale bluish or greyish ground, a particularly attractive technique known as 'white on white' or 'bianco sopra bianco' as it was of Italian origin. This type of decoration was used from about the middle of the eighteenth century at Lambeth and also at Bristol. The Lambeth delft glaze often has a warm pinky tinge.

At Bristol, from about 1650 chargers and plates were made similar to those made at Lambeth. It is sometimes extremely difficult to say exactly which pottery produced each piece. Sometimes the comparison of a piece with fragments found on the site will help in identification. The later delft designs were often painted with several colours. Green, brick red, brown, yellow and purple were used to produce rich and varied effects.

English delft drug jars are a study in themselves, only brief mention can be made here. Most of them were made at Lambeth though some were made at Liverpool; some of them bear the initials of the druggist or apothecary for whom they were made as well as the date (but dated specimens are rarer in the eighteenth century). They were of several basic shapes; for dry or powdered drugs, the jars were usually cylindrical, tapering slightly towards the base. Jars for syrups and solutions were either much the same sort of shape, only with a spout at the front and a handle at the back, or the body was rounder and the foot more splayed. The eighteenth century syrup pots became more spherical and were mounted on a gracefully splayed base. The spout was placed at the back, so that it did not interfere with the painted label or cartouche with the name of the drug on the front of the pot. The tops of the jars were slightly out-turned to allow for a covering piece of parchment to be tied over the top. The eighteenth century syrup pots were picked up by the splayed foot which made a handle superfluous. Most of the jars were painted in blue only, polychrome examples being rare.

Not very many drug jars in London survived the Great Fire of 1666, for most of them bear dates later than this. The earliest designs show Italian influence with a grotesque head at each side of the ribbon or label upon which the name of the drug is written. By the 1660's the label appears surmounted by the head and outspread wings of an angel, and this type of decoration remains a common feature until the end of the seventeenth century. It is amusing to note that the coiffeur of the angel changed with the fashion in hair styles, the earliest being a thin-haired puritan character. One even resembles Oliver Cromwell, even though

58

59

60

58 Large dish, moulded in relief copied from an original by Bernard Palissy, who took the subject from a painting by Titian called *La Fécondité*. Painted in blue, green, yellow and manganese purple. Made in Lambeth about 1665. Length 18½″. *Nottingham Museum*

59 Sauce-boat in the form of a recumbent figure of Pomona in a bath. Painted in blue, orange and manganese purple. Copied from a design by Palissy. *c.* 1650. Made in Lambeth. Length 8″. *Fitzwilliam Museum*

60 Wine cup painted in blue, orange and manganese purple with a portrait of King Charles II. Inscribed CR and IK 1677. Made in Lambeth. Height 3⅜″. *Fitzwilliam Museum*

it is dated six years after the Restoration. The later angels are drawn wearing more and more luxuriant hair until in 1697 the angel wears a full William III wig.

Towards the end of the seventeeth century *c.* 1672 designs appeared with birds and flowers and later still a cherub or a pair of cherubs make their appearance. Apollo the Healer is depicted on some of the jars dating from the middle of the seventeenth century, and some of the most important jars are painted with the arms of the Apothecaries' Company, sometimes in several colours.

Some of the drugs named on the jars sound most extraordinary. For example *O. Vulpin* or oil of foxes, which was an embrocation made from the fat of middle aged foxes, and said to be very beneficial for chest complaints.

The drug jars were made in various sizes to hold the apothecaries' stock-in-trade. Very small delft pots were made to hold such preparations as Singleton's *Golden Eye Ointment* or Jacob Hemet's *Essence of Pearl* dentifrice (this was used by George II). These little pots were inscribed in blue in a cursive hand, and were obviously made in large quantities and supplied to the makers in which to package their medicaments. The delft pill slabs were made in various shapes, some like hearts or shields, others were octagonal or oblong. Often they were decorated with the arms of the Apothecaries' Company, but rarely are they dated. They were always pierced with two little holes at the top, so that they could be hung up. As few of these show signs of having been used, it seems likely that they were made for decoration in a window or shop, or perhaps to show the customers that the apothecary was a genuine member of the Apothecaries' Company. The seventeenth century wine bottles or decanters were often dated and marked with the name of the wine Claret, Sack, Whit (*sic*) or occasionally Rhenish. They were probably made for the better class taverns or for wine merchants to use with their customers for tasting wine. It seems unlikely that the wine was actually bottled in them though the neck was grooved or ringed to enable a parchment cover to be tied over the top. Wine cups were also made, often decorated with the arms of liveried companies, a portrait of the king or even a bawdy joke.

Delft does not seem to have been made at Liverpool before the eighteenth century, at least the first known dated piece is a large plaque inscribed 'A West Prospect of Great Crosby 1716'. But the first mention of pottery at Liverpool occurs in a list of town dues payable at the port in 1674, which contains the following item:

'For every cartload of mugs (shipped) into foreign ports 6d; for every cartload of mugs along the coast 4d; for every crate of cupps or pipes along the coast 1d.'

In the *Transactions of the Historical Society of Lancashire and Cheshire*, 3 May 1855, there is an interesting account by Dr Joseph Mayer of a potter, Zachariah Barnes, making delft at Liverpool in the latter half of the eighteenth century, when its use had been superseded in most of the country by salt-glazed stoneware and later by cream-coloured earthenware. Dr Mayer wrote: 'Amongst other articles were very large round dishes, chiefly sent into Wales, where the simple habits of their forefathers remained unchanged long after their alteration in England; and the master of the house and his guests dipped their spoons into the mess and helped themselves from the dish placed in the middle of the table. Quantities of this ware were sent to the great border fairs, held at Chester, whither the inhabitants of the more remote and inaccessible parts of the mountain districts of Wales assembled, to buy their stores for the year. This continued until a very recent time. . . .'

Delft ware was made for a short time at Wincanton in Somerset from 1736 and also in the eighteenth century, in Glasgow, Dublin and Limerick.

61

62

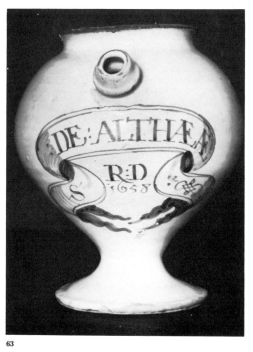

63

64

61 Unguent pot, decorated in blue and manganese purple. Made in Lambeth in the latter part of the seventeenth century. Height 4½″. *Guildhall Museum*

62 Apothecaries' pill-slab, decorated in blue. Pierced for hanging. Made in Lambeth 1663. Height 10½″. *Pharmaceutical Society*

63 Wet drug jar or syrup pot: *S de Althaeae*: syrup of marshmallow. Made from an emollient herb with soothing properties. The jar is painted in blue on a white ground. This plain ribbon design was used at the time of the Commonwealth. Made in Lambeth 1658. Height 7½″. *Pharmaceutical Society*

64 Drug jar: *Electuarium e succo rosarium*: a sweet syrup of roses. Quincy in 1724 scornfully dismisses it as being not particularly beneficial for anything and adds that it is hardly ever prescribed. A complicated design painted in blue incorporating Apollo the Healer, also an angel and peacocks. Dated 1679. Height 8⅛″. *Lothian Collection*

65

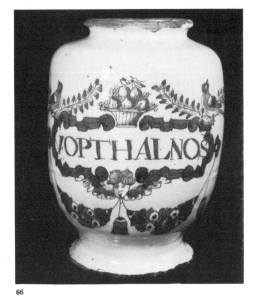
66

67

68

65 Wet drug jar: *O. Vulpin*: oil of foxes; made by boiling a fox's carcase with various herbs in wine. 'Exceeding good for pains in the joynts' according to Culpeper. The jar is painted in blue on a white ground with an angel design, much used in the late seventeenth century. Made in Lambeth 1684. Height 7½". *Collection: Dr John F. Wilkinson*

66 Drug jar: *V. Opthalnos*: an ointment for the eyes made from calamine, lead oxide and other ingredients. Painted in blue on a white ground, an example of the bird and basket design used in the early eighteenth century. Made in Lambeth. Early eighteenth century. Height 7¾". *Pharmaceutical Society*

67 Pill-slab painted in blue with the arms of the Apothecaries' company, with the lettering in manganese. A cedar of Lebanon surmounts the arms. Pierced for hanging. Made in Lambeth *c.* 1700. Height 11¼". *Pharmaceutical Society*

68 Syrup pot: *S. e Mecon*: syrup of poppies, a cough syrup containing opium. This shape of eighteenth-century syrup pot could be conveniently grasped by the narrow waist, which did away with the necessity of a handle. A design with cherubs painted in blue on a white ground. Mid-eighteenth century. Lambeth. Height 7½". *Pharmaceutical Society*

69 Barber-surgeons' dish painted in
blue with a design that
incorporates the tools of both
the barber's and the surgeon's
trade. Made in Lambeth.
c. 1690. Dia. 10⅜″. *Nottingham
Museum*

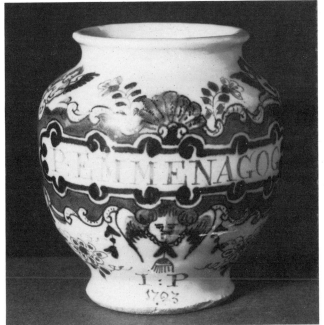

70 Pill jar: *P. Emmenagog*:
abortifacient pills. This
polychrome design is painted in
blue, red and green incorporating
cherubs. 1723. Made in
Lambeth. Height 3¼″. *Victoria
and Albert Museum*

71

72

73

74

71 Circular dish with polychrome decoration in the Italian style. The dashing horseman is probably intended to be Charles II when Prince of Wales. Made in Lambeth about 1645. Dia. $12\frac{3}{4}''$. *Fitzwilliam Museum*

72 Circular dish painted in blue and brownish orange. The back of the dish is glazed only with a transparent lead glaze. This was often the case. Made in Lambeth. *c.* 1650. Dia. $15\frac{5}{8}''$. *Fitzwilliam Museum*

73 Posset pot with lid painted in blue, after the manner of the Dutch. On one side the initials J.H. and the other the date 1700. The crownshaped lid does not belong to the pot. Made in Bristol. Height $11\frac{1}{2}''$. *Fitzwilliam Museum*

74 Vessel in the form of a man with a pipe. Painted in blue, turquoise and orange. Probably copied from a silver original. Under the base are the initials $R \; \overset{M}{} \, M$ and the date 1675. Made in Lambeth. Height $9\frac{1}{8}''$. *Fitzwilliam Museum*

75

76

77

78

75 Circular dish painted in blue with portraits of Charles II and Catherine of Braganza. The Italian influence is very noticeable. Made in Lambeth. *c.* 1662. Dia. 13″. *Victoria and Albert Museum*

76 Circular dish painted with a portrait of James II, (1685–88) painted in blue on a light greeny blue ground. There are other chargers almost identical to this one (even to the position of the eyes) marked Charles II. They were made in Lambeth between 1660 and 1700. Dia. 13¼″. *Victoria and Albert Museum*

77 Circular dish with a portrait of Mary II wife of William III (elder daughter of James II), painted in blue, yellow and manganese purple. Late 17th century. Attributed to Brislington, near Bristol. Dia. 13¼″. *Victoria and Albert Museum*

78 Circular plate with portraits of King William III and Mary II painted in blue and orange. Made in Lambeth. *c.* 1690. Dia. 8¼″. *Victoria and Albert Museum*

79

80

79 Circular dish with blue dash border and decoration in blue, olive green, yellow and black. The back of the dish is covered with a transparent greenish glaze. Early eighteenth century. Probably made in Lambeth. Dia. 13½″. *Fitzwilliam Museum*

80 Plate with a pottery kiln painted on it in blue in the Chinese style. Made in Lambeth in the mid-eighteenth century. Dia. 8¾″.

81 Punch bowl, painted in blue on a white ground. Probably made in Bristol. *c.* 1715. Dia. 10¼″. *Fitzwilliam Museum*

82 Teapot with attached lid. It would have been filled through a hole in the bottom on the inkwell principle, in the manner of the Cadogan teapots. Probably made at Joseph Flower's pottery at Bristol. *c.* 1750. Height 5⅝″. *Fitzwilliam Museum*

81
82

83   84

83 Tile painted in blue with details in green and red. Made in Bristol during the first half of the eighteenth century. 5″ sq. *Fitzwilliam Museum*

84 Tile of a pale lavender colour painted with blue and opaque white (*bianco sopra bianco*). Made by Joseph Flower in Bristol. *c.* 1760. 5″ sq. *Fitzwilliam Museum*

85 An old aquatint showing the Thames side in the eighteenth century. A potter's kiln is plainly visible near the Lambeth foreshore on the left. This is probably one of the delft potteries. *Doulton and Co Ltd*

85

86

86 Mug probably painted by John Bowen at the Flower pottery. Blue painting with a red line round the rim, below which is the inscription 'MARY TURNER AGED 2 YEARS 14 DAYS SEPr 2 1752. Height 3¾″. *Fitzwilliam Museum*

87 Punch bowl with the inscription inside 'One bowl more and then'. Painted outside in blue, yellow and purple. Made in Lambeth. *c.* 1760. Dia. 10½″.
Flower brick, painted in purple, blue, yellow and green. Made in Liverpool. *c.* 1760. 3⅛″ high.
Plate painted in blue and manganese purple. Made in Bristol. *c.* 1760. Dia. 9¼″. *Victoria and Albert Museum*

87

88 Punch bowl painted in blue, yellow, brownish red, manganese purple and green. Made in Liverpool about 1760. Dia. 14″. *Fitzwilliam Museum*

89 Circular dish painted in blue, green, reddish brown and yellow. The Fall was a very popular subject for illustration. Made in Bristol. *c.* 1730. Dia. 13″. *Collection : Edwin Rideout*

90

91

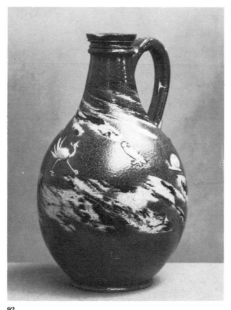

92

93

90 Stoneware bust of Prince Rupert by John Dwight of Fulham, made about 1672–80. Height 24″. *British Museum*

91 Light coloured stoneware bust by John Dwight, said to be Elizabeth, wife of Samuel Pepys. As she had died in 1669, it seems unlikely he could have modelled it from life. Possibly Pepys commissioned Dwight to make it after her death. Late seventeenth century. Height $6\frac{7}{8}″$. *British Museum*

92 Jug decorated with marbling and stamped ornaments. Made at the Fulham potteries about 1680. Height $7\frac{1}{2}″$. *Victoria and Albert Museum*

93 Bellarmine jug made during the last quarter of the seventeenth century, probably at Dwight's Fulham factory. Height $10\frac{3}{4}″$. *Guildhall Museum*

4 Stoneware

Stoneware is made from clay to which a certain amount of sand has been added.
It is fired at a higher temperature than ordinary earthenware, so that it becomes
partly vitrified and impervious to liquids. It was sometimes glazed with common
salt, which was thrown into the kiln when it was at full heat. The salt volatilized
and reacted on the water vapour in the kiln to form a coating of silicate of soda,
which gave the ware its characteristic orange peel texture. It was first made in
the Middle Ages in Germany on the Lower Rhine and quantities of this ware
were imported into England in the sixteenth and seventeenth centuries.

Stoneware was first made in this country in 1672, when John Dwight MA Oxon.
at one time secretary to the Bishop of Chester, founded the Fulham Pottery. In
the previous year Dwight had obtained a warrant from Charles II for making
'Transparent earthenware or china and stoneware vulgarly called Cologne ware'.
At Fulham, Dwight started by making copies of the German wine jugs, which
had a bearded face on the front. These were commonly called Greybeards or
Bellarmines, after Cardinal Bellarmine, whose controversial writings had so up-
set the Reformed Church in the Netherlands.

Dwight also modelled some quite remarkable portrait busts in hard drab grey
stoneware; among them were portraits of King Charles II, Prince Rupert and a
charming lady said to be Mrs Pepys (though that lady had actually died in 1669).
He also modelled his own infant daughter lying upon her death bed, and he cast
her tiny hand in stoneware.

John Dwight also made jugs and mugs and other vessels in clays which had
been mingled together to resemble agate, as well as red clay teapots in imitation
of the Chinese Yi Hsing ware that was then being imported into this country in
the chests of tea. He never succeeded in making porcelain.

In 1693 Dwight put in hand lawsuits against a number of potters for infringing
his patent. Amongst them were four potters: Wedgwood of Burslem, the two
brothers Elers of Bradwell and James Morley of Nottingham. The results of
the litigation are not known, but it proves that there was a connection between
Dwight and the Elers. Dwight died in 1703, but the Fulham pottery was carried
on by his family.

HARD UNGLAZED RED STONEWARE OF THE ELERS TYPE

The brothers John and Philip Elers came over to England at about the same time
as William of Orange in 1688. Although they were said to be of aristocratic birth,
they had both learned a good deal about the craft of pottery-making both in

94   95

94 Drab coloured stoneware jug, the upper part mottled brown. Made at Fulham in the late seventeenth century. Height 3⅞". *Fitzwilliam Museum*

95 Brown stoneware figure of a cock with incised decoration. Made at Fulham in the late eighteenth century. Height 9". *Fitzwilliam Museum*

RED STONEWARE

96 Pear-shaped coffee pot in the hard red unglazed stoneware of the Elers' type, decorated with sprigged patterns in the Elers' manner. The numbers 45 appear on the shield. Made in Staffordshire. Mid-eighteenth century. Height 8½". *Fitzwilliam Museum*

97 Pear-shaped coffee pot in unglazed red stoneware with engine-turned decoration and a simulated Chinese impressed mark on the base. *c.* 1765. Height 9". *City Museum, Stoke-on-Trent*

96   97

98 Teapot made of the Elers' type of red stoneware with sprigged decoration of prunus blossom. Made in Staffordshire in the late seventeenth century. Height 4½″. *Victoria and Albert Museum*

Delft and Cologne. However, they must have been very versatile craftsmen for on arrival in England they at first practised as silversmiths. Possibly inspired by the obviously increasing need for teapots, cups and saucers (resulting from the ever growing habit of tea drinking) they decided to set up a pottery to make 'fine red porcelain'. On Dwight's advice they went to Staffordshire and started a pottery in Bradwell Wood, where there was a deposit of red clay. In this project they had the assistance of John Chandler, one of Dwight's exworkmen.

The Elers red ware was not porcelain at all, but a very fine stoneware, with a dense, red, semi-vitrified body. The fine quality was achieved by intensely careful preparation of the clay, and the hardness by the high temperature at which it was fired. The pieces were thrown and then turned upon a lathe. Any decoration was applied as a dab of clay which was then pressed with a metal die, made in the form of a leaf or flower, any surplus clay was then very carefully cleared away. Spouts and handles were usually modelled by hand. The Elers must have taken infinite care at every stage of production and the ware was always beautifully finished. They did not actually mark their ware with their names, but many of their pieces bear pseudo-Chinese stamps on the base. It was certainly not cheap, their red teapots sold for 10s to 25s each in London, where David Elers opened up a warehouse in the Poultry.

It seems that the Elers were also responsible for introducing salt-glazing into Staffordshire, for it is reported that 'Eight Burslem potters assembled round the Elers' new ovens to protest at the volumes of smoke they emitted.'★

The Elers left Staffordshire in 1710, by which time they had introduced not only the fine red stoneware and salt-glazing, but a black ware similar to the later black basalt ware of Josiah Wedgwood. They had also introduced many technical improvements, such as the use of the lathe, metal stamps, alabaster moulds and the refining of clays. They always worked under conditions of great secrecy employing only workmen who appeared to be dull witted. However, two young

★*The History of Manchester :* Aikin : 1794

53

99

100

101

99 Posset pot of a light yellowish-brown stoneware. The lower part has a pierced outer casing. The upper part bears on one side the royal arms in moulded relief and on the other side, divided by the spout, the legend   Samuel Watkinson   Major   Sarah Watkinson   Majoress of Nottingham
                                     1700
This is the earliest dated piece of Nottingham stoneware. Height 10½″. *Nottingham Museum*

100 Jug (or perhaps a tobacco jar) in the form of a bear. The surface is covered in small shavings of clay. Made in Nottingham in the eighteenth century. Height 10¼″. *Nottingham Museum*

101 Two mugs, the one on the left inscribed 'Joseph Boot 1748'. Height 4¾″ and the other dated 1720. Height 4¼″. *Nottingham Museum*

102 James Morley's trade card. Engraved about 1690. This was the James Morley who John Dwight had taken proceedings against in 1693, for infringing his copyright. *Bodleian Library*

A Decantor   A Flower-Pot   A Carved Teapot   A Capuchine   A Mogg   A Carved Jug

Such as have Occation for these Sorts of Pots commonly called Stone-Ware, or for such as are of any other Shape not here Represented may be furnished w.th them by the Maker James Morley at ỹ Pot-House in Nottingham

102

Staffordshire potters, John Astbury and Josiah Twyford—so the story goes—worked for two years for the Elers, pretending all the time to be half-wits, while absorbing all the Elers' knowledge and skill.

NOTTINGHAM STONEWARE

A fine brown salt-glazed stoneware was made in Nottingham throughout the eighteenth century. The earliest dated piece is 1700, the latest is 1799. This salt-glazed ware was covered with a wash of ferruginous clay, which burnt to an irridescent brown sheen. It was made by the Morleys of Mughouse Lane—the same Morley against whom Dwight took proceedings in 1693, and whose trade card appears above.

Nottingham ware was carefully thrown, then turned on the lathe. Any decorations such as scrolls or leaves and inscriptions, were scratched on to the unfired clay surface with a sharp point. The handles were usually made by hand. Typical pieces were loving-cups, puzzle-jugs, mugs and punch bowls. Curious jugs in the shape of a bear were also made, the surface of these was covered in clay shavings to represent fur. Bear baiting was a popular, if revolting, sport in the eighteenth century. Later in the early nineteenth century, bear jugs were made with a political significance, the Russian bear hugging Napoleon to his chest in a deadly embrace.

Similar brown salt-glazed stoneware was also made at Chesterfield and Brampton, though the Nottingham ware was superior in quality to any of its rivals. In fact, the quality of Nottingham stoneware remains of an extraordinary high standard throughout the entire period of its production.

103
104

105

106

103 Teapot with incised decoration and a twisted
handle. Made in Nottingham about 1750.
Height 5½″. *Nottingham Museum*

104 Teapot decorated with bands of incised lines
and crumbled clay particles. Made in
Nottingham about 1790. Height 5⅛″.
Nottingham Museum

105 Punch bowl with incised decoration made in
Nottingham in 1750. Height 12¾″. *Victoria and
Albert Museum*

106 Toby jug made at Brampton at the beginning
of the nineteenth century. The Brampton
stoneware is quite often, understandably,
mistaken for the Nottingham stoneware. Height
12″. *Nottingham Museum*

107

108

109

STONEWARE OF JOHN DOULTON IN THE EARLY
NINETEENTH CENTURY

John Doulton, who was born at Fulham in 1793, was apprenticed to the pottery that John Dwight had founded. At that time the pottery was making strictly utilitarian wares such as ink and blacking bottles* and jars for spirits and chemicals, though they also made mugs and jugs decorated in relief with hunting scenes.

After finishing his apprenticeship, John Doulton, who had become a very expert craftsman, went into partnership with Martha Jones and John Watts. Mrs Jones retired in 1820 and the firm became Doulton and Watts. Due to the extremely hard work of both partners the firm began to expand; by the middle of the nineteenth century it had become the largest and best known manufacturer of chemical stoneware in Europe.

As well as the utilitarian pipes, chimney pots and water filters, the firm made decorative flasks and jugs with the likenesses of Nelson and other famous people. In 1835 Henry (John Doulton's second son) then aged fifteen had joined the family business and proved himself to be not only an extremely good technician but an inventive man as well. It was through his inventiveness that steam was harnessed to drive the potters' wheels. When John Watts retired in 1854 the firm became Doulton and Co.

Up to the mid-1860's the firm had not really concerned itself very much with producing decorative wares, but Henry Doulton became interested in the Lambeth School of Art and many of its students came to work at the Doulton pottery. The enduring effect this had on the production of decorative stoneware will be referred to later in the section on the artist potters of the later nineteenth century.

*It was Doulton and Watts's blacking bottles that Charles Dickens remembered labelling by the hundred, during his childhood when he was working at Warrens' warehouse near Hungerford Stairs.

107 Brown salt-glazed stoneware mug depicting Admiral Nelson. Made by Doulton and Watts at Lambeth. *c.* 1820. Height 8″. *Royal Doulton Potteries*

108 Salt-glazed stoneware filter. Made by Doulton and Watts. *c.* 1854. Height approx. 24″. *Royal Doulton Potteries*

109 Brown salt-glazed stoneware 'Reform' bottle. Flask made to contain 'The true Spirit of Reform'. Made by Doulton and Watts, Lambeth 1832. Height 14″. *Royal Doulton Potteries*

110
111

110 Drab salt-glazed stoneware with applied white pipeclay decoration. Sometimes called 'Crouch' ware, said to have been made by Dr Thomas Wedgwood, who died in 1737. c. 1720. Height 4½″.

111 Almost white salt-glazed bowl with sprigged on decoration. Made to commemorate the taking of Porto Bello by Admiral Vernon in 1739. Made in Staffordshire. Width 5¼″. *Willett Collection, Brighton*

5 Salt-glazed stoneware

In the early years of the eighteenth century, a number of Staffordshire potters were experimenting with various ways of producing a ware comparable to the fine Chinese porcelain that was then being imported into the country. The manufacturers of delft ware had done their best, but the tin-enamelled earthenware chipped and scratched easily. The potters were trying to find a ware that was white and reasonably thin and fragile-looking, while retaining great strength and if possible it had to be translucent. The latter quality the salt-glazed potters never achieved.

Taking a lead from the work of John Dwight of Fulham, they turned their attention to the manufacture of a light-coloured salt-glazed stoneware.

Dr Thomas Wedgwood, working in Staffordshire in 1710 was known to have made a buff-coloured salt-glazed stoneware decorated with raised designs made of white pipeclay. This is sometimes known as 'Crouch' ware.

About 1720, John Astbury, who had worked with the Elers, perfected a white body by adding calcined flints to a light coloured clay mixture. This resulted in a ware that was both hard and strong. Astbury failed to produce the translucency of porcelain, but had invented a fine stoneware that could be moulded with very great precision. Very soon a number of Staffordshire potters were also making white salt-glazed stoneware, and it was said that when the kilns were being fired, the entire neighbourhood was plunged into smoky darkness, caused by the action of the salt when thrown into the red hot kilns.

Until about 1730, plates and simple shapes were made by taking a 'bat' of clay and pressing it into or on to a mould. There was a limit to the thinness of ware that could be achieved by this method, so when the demand grew for teapots and sauceboats and other complicated shapes, a new method had to be invented, and this was the casting of the ware in a mould.

The moulds were first of all made of Derbyshire alabaster, and a highly skilled job it was to make them. Later, about 1745, plaster of Paris moulds were introduced from France.

The original alabaster or plaster mould was kept as a master copy and further plaster copies were made from this as working moulds. The porous mould, in two or more pieces, was assembled, and the clay, mixed with water to form slip was poured into the mould. This was left to stand for a few minutes while the porous mould absorbed water from the slip, depositing against the sides of the mould a thin layer of solid clay. Then the superfluous slip was poured off and when the clay was sufficiently dry, the mould could be removed from the thin clay casting.

Tableware of all kinds was made in salt-glazed stoneware, decorated with intricate patterns of raised basket-work or rococo scroll forms, often with pierced borders. The crisp precision of the moulding of these patterns is the most remarkable feature of this ware. Aaron Wood, who had been apprenticed to Dr Thomas Wedgwood, was one of the most famous of the early block-cutters, as the mould-makers were called. He was certainly responsible for cutting intricate patterns for moulds for tableware and it has been suggested that he made a number of the early pew groups.

Colour was first introduced by incising a design into the body of the ware, in its leather-hard state, and then rubbing cobalt-stained clay into the indentations. This technique dates from the 1740's and the ware is known as 'scratch blue'.

About 1750 coloured enamelling was used with great success. The colours were painted on over the glaze and the ware was then re-fired in a muffle kiln. Often these enamel colours have an exceptionally clear and jewel-like quality. Salt-glazed teapots were often made in the most fantastic shapes: houses, camels and even pecten shells. Teapots of a more orthodox shape were painted with enamel colours in many different designs including somewhat naive attempts at oriental landscapes and figures. Patterns were painted incorporating birds, flowers, feathers, portraits of the King of Prussia and the Young Pretender hiding in an oak tree.

Primitive figures were made, either as toys or for ornament. Some of these took the form of a group of figures sitting on a settle or a pew. These were white but picked out here and there with dark brown clay for such details as shoes, eyes and buttons. Other figures, both human and animal, including some very spirited mounted soldiers were also made in white salt-glazed stoneware.

Agate ware was also used with a salt glaze, both for teapots and for figures. The ware was made of white and dark brown clay carefully cut and blended to resemble agate. Sometimes blue was added as well.

Enamel coloured salt-glazed figures are extremely rare and lack the charm of the simpler white and brown ones.

By about 1770, the manufacture of salt-glazed stoneware had almost ceased, cream-coloured earthenware having become firmly established by that date. Unfortunately salt-glazed stoneware is never marked with the name of a maker, though there are still some moulds in existence signed with the maker's name.

112 White salt-glazed horseman with details picked out in dark brown clay. Made in Staffordshire. *c.* 1730. Height 9¼". *Victoria and Albert Museum*

112

113
114

113 White salt-glazed pew group, with details in dark brown clay. Made in Staffordshire. *c.* 1730. Height 6″. *Fitzwilliam Museum*

114 White salt-glazed pew group, with details in dark brown clay. Made in Staffordshire. *c.* 1730. Height 6¼″. *British Museum*

115
117

116
118

115 White salt-glazed moulded figures. Made in Staffordshire. *c*. 1750. Height 7¼″. *Fitzwilliam Museum*

116 Salt-glazed figure in white and brown agate ware, touched with splashes of blue. Made in Staffordshire. *c*. 1740. Height 4½″. *Fitzwilliam Museum*

117 Salt-glazed salt cellar, made in Staffordshire and dated 1744. Height 3″. *British Museum*

118 Salt-glazed jelly mould, made in Staffordshire. *c*. 1740. Height 1¼″. *Victoria and Albert Museum*

119

120

119 Moulded salt-glazed teapot in the form of a camel, made in Staffordshire about 1745. Height 6¼″. *Fitzwilliam Museum*

120 Teapot in the form of a house with a dolphin spout and scaley handle. Made in Staffordshire. *c.* 1740. Height 4¼″.

121

122

121 Salt-glazed plate with moulded decoration. Made in Staffordshire by Aaron Wood *c*. 1760 (an inscription by Enoch Wood dated 1836 on the back testifies to this). Dia. 17″.

122 White salt-glazed plate with an elaborately moulded and pierced design painted with a polychrome pseudo-Chinese design. *c*. 1760. Dia. 12″.

123 Pear-shaped white salt-glazed jug. Painted with a portrait of Prince Charles Edward Stuart in a rococo scrolled frame, and bouquets of thistles and roses. Made in Staffordshire. *c.* 1765. Height 8¼″. *Victoria and Albert Museum*

124 Puzzle jug with incised decoration coloured with cobalt. This technique is known as 'scratch blue'. Made in Staffordshire and dated 1764. Height 10″. *Victoria and Albert Museum*

125 Jug of salt-glazed stoneware with incised and impressed decoration, painted in blue. The initials are those of George III. Made in Staffordshire about 1770. Height 13″. *Victoria and Albert Museum*

126 'Scratch blue' mug. Inscribed IH 1752. Staffordshire. Height 5″. *Victoria and Albert Museum*

127

128

127 White salt-glazed moulded teapot painted with a design of oakleaves and Chinese flowers. The figure at the top of the shell is meant to represent Bonnie Prince Charlie. Made in Staffordshire. *c.* 1745. Height 5½".

128 White salt-glazed teapot painted with oriental flowers in brilliant enamel colours, green, pink, yellow and turquoise blue. Made in Staffordshire. *c.* 1760.

129

129 White salt-glazed teapot decorated with
enamel colours. Bird subjects like pigeons
are unusual on salt-glazed stoneware.
Made in Staffordshire about 1760.
Height 4½″.

130 Pair of birds, modelled in salt-glazed
stoneware, decorated in brilliant enamel
colours. Made in Staffordshire about
1760. *British Museum*

130

131

132

133

134

131 Sugar-box in hard white unglazed stoneware decorated with blue lines and a polychrome landscape in a medallion. Marked TURNER impressed. *c.* 1780. Height 4½″.

132 Castleford teapot made of hard white stoneware with embossed decoration in part outlined in blue. Marked D D & Co CASTLEFORD. *c.* 1795. Height 4¾″. *Victoria and Albert Museum*

133 Jug in hard white unglazed stoneware of the Castleford type, painted in very bright enamel colours, blue, turquoise and red and green predominating. The subject (impressed) 'Mischievous Sport' is from an almost identical mould as the Pratt type jug illustrated on page 119. Probably made at Castleford, but unmarked. *c.* 1800. Height 4⅝″.

134 An unmarked, but unmistakeably Castleford type of stoneware jug, decorated with a typical 'Pratt' subject: Lord Garvis (sic). The only colouring is a rich blue for the bands and a pale green for the leaves. Very similar, but not identical to the jug on page 119. *c.* 1797. Height 4½″. *Collection: Geoffrey A. Godden*

135 Two teapots with sliding lids of typical Castleford shape and design. Both are outlined in blue and the one on the right has a landscape painted in various colours. Both specimens are unmarked. The taller of the two pots is 6⅜″ high. Very probably made by David Dunderdale at Castleford. *c.* 1795.

WHITE STONEWARE OF THE CASTLEFORD TYPE, LATE EIGHTEENTH AND EARLY NINETEENTH CENTURY

Still in the same tradition of moulded stoneware, an interesting and until quite recently somewhat neglected type was made during the last twenty years of the eighteenth and the first twenty years of the nineteenth centuries. This had a very hard, dense, white almost porcellanous body which was vitrified rather than glazed.

Though John Turner had been experimenting with this kind of ware in the 1780's and had made many moulded pieces with relief decoration, including some with blue lines added (see page 72), the name so often given to this type of ware is 'Castleford'.

A factory was started at Castleford, not far from Leeds, in about 1790 by David Dunderdale. Jugs and teapots, some with sliding lids, were made here in this very hard, white stoneware. A few specimens are marked D D & Co Castleford Pottery, but marked pieces are rare. They have an extremely crisp and precise quality and the relief modelling shows up to great advantage. (As they are non-shiny they photograph well, unlike the underglaze coloured Pratt ware, with which they have something in common from the design point of view.)

These Castleford teapots were usually decorated with blue lines edging the panels in which the design was worked out, occasionally a rather crude bright green was used as well. Sometimes even more rarely, several colours were used (see the jug on page 72). Occasionally a little landscape was painted in several colours on a medallion on the side of the teapot. Though many pieces remain unmarked, the marks of other potters which have been found on similar ware include Clulow and Co of Fenton (*c.* 1802); Heath and Son of Burslem (*c.* 1797); Benjamin Plant of Longton (*c.* 1780–1820) and Sowter and Co of Mexborough (1795–1804).

135

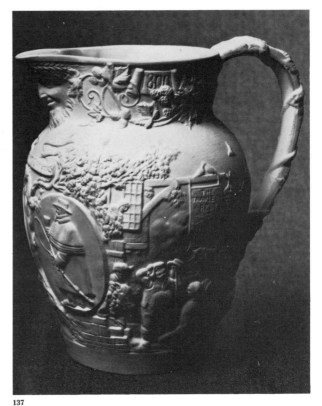

136
138

136 Octagonal white stoneware jug, moulded in relief with eight figures of religious significance in gothic niches. Designed by Charles Meigh of Hanley and registered at the Patent Office Design Registry on March 17 1848. Height 6¼". *Victoria and Albert Museum*

137 The Two Drivers jug, moulded in relief in white stoneware. The design by Henry Townsend shows the old fashioned coach driver with cape and whip on one side and the modern engine driver with his locomotive on the other side. Made originally for Sir Henry Cole's Summerly's Art Manufactures. Made by Mintons, inscribed underneath No 335 M. *c.* 1847. Height 7". (For a similar jug, showing different colouring and reverse side see page 151.)

138 White stoneware mug moulded in relief with a pattern of vines and dancing figures. The design was adapted by Charles Meigh from the picture *Bacchanalian Dance* by Nicholas Poussin. 1847. Height 7¼".

Before leaving white stoneware for an entirely new subject, it seems an appropriate place to finish the white stoneware story, although somewhat out of chronological sequence.

After the Castleford type of ware ceased to be made, white stoneware was used for a different purpose and this was for the making of decorative jugs. These, until recently, have been dismissed as Victorian monstrosities but at last they are beginning to be appreciated.

In these white stoneware jugs of the 1835–70 period it is possible to see all the vulgarity and verve and gusto of the nineteenth century as well as the piety and sentimentality. These stoneware jugs were moulded in high relief and the patterns were richly and flamboyantly embossed with subjects ranging from gothic settings of biblical scenes to Bacchanalian revels and classical tableaux, while others were encrusted with plant forms of every description from vines to bulrushes.

The basic shapes of the jugs themselves were enormously varied and range from angular, octagonal, straight-sided jugs on a foot, to bulging-bellied and decanter-shaped jugs and even jugs tapering slightly towards the top and resembling plant-encrusted logs of wood. Almost every square inch of these jugs was thick with decoration, elaborate handles and lips added to the richness of the design. They present a wonderful challenge to the collector, for they are still comparatively easy to find. They must have been made in very large quantities.

Many of these jugs are marked with the name of the maker, some of them can be precisely dated for they were registered at the Patent Office Design Registry and are marked with the appropriate mark. This mark is a diamond shaped device with Class IV at the top (for ceramics) and from the years 1847–67 the year of registration is signified by a letter in the top corner of the diamond; the month by another letter to the left of the diamond and the precise day of the month is indicated in the right hand corner. The parcel number appears at the bottom. These date tables can be found in various reference books including Wakefield's *Victorian Pottery* and G. A. Godden's *Encyclopaedia of British Pottery and Porcelain Marks* (both published by Herbert Jenkins).

These jugs were made by many different makers including William Ridgway & Co of Hanley, and Ridgway and Abington. Edward John Ridgway was the son of William Ridgway who went into partnership with Leonard Abington, who was the modeller responsible for the design of the jugs. T. & R. Boote of Burslem made straight-sided jugs tapering very slightly towards the top – the forerunner of the plain tankard shaped jugs in common use today. Charles Meigh in the 1840's was probably the most accomplished of the 'gothic' designers and his jugs have a balance and symmetry lacking in many of the later designs. Cork and Edge, T. J. & J. Mayer, Holland and Green, J. & M. P. Bell, Mintons and Copelands are among the many names that are to be found upon these white stoneware jugs.

139 Horseman modelled in different coloured clays and glazed with an almost colourless lead glaze. Made in Staffordshire. *c.* 1740. Height 7″. *Victoria and Albert Museum*

6 Lead-glazed red earthenware

ALSO TORTOISESHELL, AGATE AND MARBLED WARE OF THE
EIGHTEENTH CENTURY

At the same time that white salt-glazed stoneware was being made, other potters were experimenting with earthenware bodies and coloured glazes. For some time during the eighteenth century the body of the ware remained much the same, whether it was to be glazed with salt or lead, but by about 1740 manufacturers tended to specialize in the use of either one glaze or the other and experiments went on to find the most suitable clay mixture for use with each type of glaze.

The most famous potters concerned with these developments were Astbury (who had worked with the Elers), his son Thomas, Thomas Whieldon and Enoch Booth.

As we have seen, Astbury was something of an innovator, not only did he introduce ground calcined flints into the body of the stoneware used with salt-glaze, but he is said to have been the first potter to have imported white clay from Devonshire into Staffordshire. (It was all brought on the backs of pack animals).

Astbury and his son made red, brown and black fine thin earthenware rather like that made by the Elers, but the Astburys ornamented their ware with sprigged decorations made of white pipeclay and they used a fine silky lead glaze, which gave a pleasantly smooth finish to their tablewares. Sometimes the ware was only decorated with a simple band of white slip. They did not mark their wares, but factory wasters of this red or brown ware have been found on the site of the old Astbury works. The same kind of ware was also made by other potters in the Stoke-on-Trent district, for many other sites have yielded similar pottery. So the term 'Astbury' can only apply loosely to indicate the type of pottery, and not specifically to state the maker.

Figures of musicians and soldiers modelled in different coloured clays have also been attributed to the Astburys. The father died in 1743, and his son later made fine cream-coloured earthenware.

Lead glazing had always been a dangerous process, as the oxide of lead was used in powder form, causing lead poisoning to the people working with it. However, by about 1740, Enoch Booth had perfected a fluid glaze in which the dangerous lead powder was ground up in water with flint and clay. The ware to be glazed was then dipped into this after it had been fired to the biscuit state. The liquid glaze clung to the porous biscuit in an even coating, and the pieces were then refired.

Some time before 1740, Thomas Whieldon is known to have been making knife handles for the Sheffield cutlers. These were made by blending together different coloured clays to make an agate-like ware. Later he experimented in the use of coloured glazes which he mixed in various ways in imitation of tortoiseshell. The colours he used were yellow, brown, green, blue and grey from the oxides of iron, manganese, copper and cobalt. Most of the so-called Whieldon ware is either brownish or greenish, and the other colours are sometimes added as large blotches.

The block-cutter Aaron Wood had worked for Whieldon for a time from 1746, and a number of young men who worked for him as apprentices afterwards distinguished themselves. Amongst these was Josiah Spode. It is recorded of him 'He is to receive 2s 3d a week, or 2s 6d if he deserves it'.

In 1754, Whieldon took as a partner young Josiah Wedgwood. While working with Whieldon, Wedgwood invented a fine green glaze which was used to decorate wares in all kinds of fanciful shapes such as cauliflowers and pine-apples. Together they continued to make agate, marbled and tortoiseshell pieces. The partners continued to refine the earthenware body that they were using under the tortoiseshell glazes, until Wedgwood felt it was good enough to stand on its own merits, without the need for covering up with a dark glaze. In 1759, the partnership came to an end. Wedgwood started up on his own and began to make the cream-coloured earthenware for which he became so famous. He introduced this in 1761.

Whieldon continued to make his variegated wares until the demand for them became less and less. He finally retired in 1780. A great many earthenware potteries during the period 1740–80 made tortoiseshell ware and as it is never marked, it is really quite impossible to say who made it. It is only safe to use the term Whieldon ware as a generic term.

Whieldon's pottery was a thatched building, as indeed all the potteries were up until the 1760's, for they were all very small, only consisting of a pot oven or kiln and a few sheds. It was not until Wedgwood built Etruria that the potteries became factories in the modern sense of the word. But before going on to consider the achievements of Josiah Wedgwood we must first have a look at the coloured glaze figures of the Woods.

140

141

142

140, 141, 142
Astbury/Whieldon type figures of musicians, modelled in different coloured clays, some of them glazed with an almost colourless lead glaze, some with a tortoiseshell glaze. Made in Staffordshire. *c.* 1740. Average height 6″. *Willett Collection, Brighton*

143

144

145

146

143 Staffordshire red-ware teapot of the Astbury type with a design in white pipeclay covered with a pale strawcoloured glaze. The lid is of a later date. *c.* 1740. Height 5″.

144 Tortoiseshell ware teapot of the Whieldon type with manganese purple-brown coloured glaze. Made in Staffordshire. *c.* 1755. Height 4½″.

145 Black-brown bodied lead-glazed teapot with the crabstock handle and spout and applied vine leaf decorations in white clay. Made in Staffordshire. *c.* 1760. Height 4¼″.

146 Diminutive Staffordshire teapot modelled after an oriental original and decorated with coloured glazes, green, manganese brown and yellow. *c.* 1755. Height 2″. *Victoria and Albert Museum*

147 Horseman and lady glazed with a brown, green and grey tortoiseshell glaze. Made in Staffordshire. *c.* 1740. Height 7½″. *Victoria and Albert Museum*

148

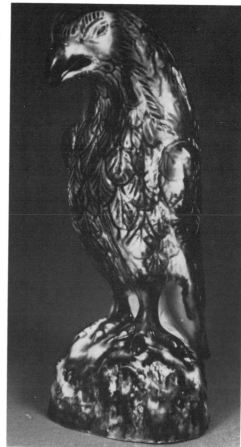

149

150

148 Whieldon-type earthenware dovecot, mottled with green, brown, yellow and black. Made in Staffordshire. *c.* 1755. Height $4\frac{7}{8}''$. *City Museum, Stoke-on-Trent*

149 Whieldon-type earthenware figure of a hawk standing on a brown and cream rocky base. Green, cream and brown tortoiseshell glaze. Made in Staffordshire. *c.* 1755. Height $7\frac{3}{4}''$. *City Museum, Stoke-on-Trent*

150 Tortoiseshell glaze plate of the Whieldon type with brown and green colouring. The moulded border design incorporates the words 'Success to the King of Prussia and his Forces'. This popular ally against the French was much commemorated on English pottery. Made in Staffordshire. *c.* 1745. Dia. $9\frac{1}{2}''$. *Willett Collection, Brighton*

82

151

151 Whieldon-type wall vase with a very pale grey-green tortoiseshell glaze. Made in Staffordshire. *c.* 1760. Height 6½″.

152

153

154

152 Agate ware teapot made of white and light red clay, lead glazed. Made in Staffordshire. *c.* 1745. Height 5¼″. *Fitzwilliam Museum*

153 Cat modelled in dark red, buff and white clays to form an agate ware. Glazed with a yellowish lead glaze. Made in Staffordshire. *c.* 1750. Height 6¾″. *Fitzwilliam Museum*

154 Handleless teacup and saucer and mugs, decorated with different kinds of agate ware bands. Made in Leeds. *c.* 1800. Dia. of saucer 5″. *Victoria and Albert Museum*

155 Earthenware group of a man and his dog, decorated in coloured glazes in the Whieldon tortoiseshell manner. *c.* 1755–60. Height 6½″. *Victoria and Albert Museum*

156 Group known as Ralph Wood and his son. The late Herbert Read says it was probably modelled by John Voyez and dates it *c.* 1770. As the elder Ralph Wood died in 1772 and as his son would have been 26 in 1770, there seem to be discrepancies. The figures are certainly decorated with coloured glazes and there is no doubt that they came from the Wood pottery. Height 8¼″.

7 The two Ralph Woods

The most important makers of earthenware figures and Toby jugs in the second half of the eighteenth century were the Woods. Ralph Wood (born 1715) and his son of the same name.

Ralph Wood the elder, was the brother of Aaron, the mouldmaker, and they were both sons of a miller of Chedleston. The miller apprenticed both his sons to potters, Ralph to John Astbury in about 1730, and Aaron to Dr Thomas Wedgwood.

Ralph Wood, after his apprenticeship was over, went to work with Thomas Whieldon, who was one of the best potters of the time. While he was with Whieldon he made salt-glazed stoneware and then the tortoiseshell glazed ware of the Astbury/Whieldon type. No doubt he was responsible for some of the early coloured glaze figures, but none of them are marked.

It seems a little uncertain exactly when Ralph Wood started to make the figures for which he is now famous, probably during the 1750's. No doubt he was helped by his brother Aaron, but the early history of the Woods seems somewhat conjectural. Falkner gives tantalisingly little solid factual information.*

The figures were well but rather simply modelled in cream-coloured earthenware, and though the Woods used the same oxide stained glazes that Whieldon had developed, they contrived to keep the colours separate by painting them carefully on to the figures with a brush, instead of allowing the colours to mingle together like tortoiseshell. Some of the figures were glazed only with a colourless lead glaze. The Woods were the first English figure makers to mark their wares with impressed names, and they sometimes added the mould number of the figure as well. In spite of this a great many figures got by without being marked at all.

Ralph's son, who was born in 1748 (died 1795) went to work with his father in the 1760's. He also became a skilled figure maker and though he used the same coloured glazes, his later work was decorated with enamel colours.

The earlier Wood figures are said to be of peasants, haymakers, sportsmen and the like and the mark used by the elder Ralph Wood is said to be R. WOOD. The younger Ralph is said to have marked his models Ra WOOD. A rebus mark in the form of a group of trees was also occasionally used.

The figures vary in subject and complexity, there are some beautifully modelled equestrian figures of such different characters as William III, St George and Hudibras; there are contemporary portrait figures such as Alderman Sir William Beckford (who was Lord Mayor of London in 1762 and again in 1769) and there are some somewhat satyrical groups such as the Vicar and Moses. There are classical figures of Jupiter, Apollo, Venus, Neptune and others; allegorical figures

*The Wood Family of Burslem: Falkner, F.: London, 1912

such as Charity and also a good many animals, deer, dogs, goats, rams, lions and even an elephant.

All the human figures have two things in common in their modelling, large hands and well-defined, slightly bulging eyes. To the elder Ralph Wood has been attributed the introduction of the Toby jug, though jugs in human form were known in mediaeval times (see page 18), and even some of the Romano-British cinerary urns had faces.

The Toby as modelled by R. WOOD was an immediate success. Hundreds of them must have been made, and they were copied by dozens of different potters from that day to this. Nobody seems to know exactly when the first one appeared; if it was inspired by Uncle Toby in *Tristram Shandy* this book was published in 1760, but if inspired by a 'pop' song called the Brown Jug, dedicated to Toby Philpot, this was written in 1761.

Many more Toby Jugs are marked with the Ra WOOD mark than with that supposedly used by the father, but very many more of them are unmarked. The personalities of these jugs are many and varied; apart from the usual stout, bucolic character with the bulbous nose, there were many slightly more refined types: Prince Hal, Lord Howe, the Squire, the Thin Man. Then there were the Welshman with his goat, the Sailor, and the Planter. There is even a formidable female version in the person of Martha Gunn, the Brighton bathing woman.

The modeller John Voyez, brought to Staffordshire by Josiah Wedgwood in 1768, had a somewhat chequered career. There are many theories that he modelled some of the Woods figures for them, but there are no signed figures to testify to this. The only model with John Voyez's signature and the Wood type of glazes is a piece known as the 'Fair Hebe' jug, a somewhat uncouth rustic jug in the form of a tree trunk with figures grouped round it. This is actually dated 1788, six years after the elder Ralph Wood had died, and the modelling has not really a very close affinity with the Wood figures. The same piece occurs with R.M. Astbury's mark and also with the initials R.G. and there are numerous later versions in enamel colours.

The younger Ralph's cousin, Enoch (the son of Aaron) was also a highly skilled modeller and potter, but as his work was more concerned with enamel colours, it is referred to in a later chapter.

157　Apollo, with green drapery and a yellow lyre. This figure has the rare rebus mark on the base (left hand side). This group of trees was the 'Wood' mark. Made between 1750–85. Height 8⅛″. *City Museum, Stoke-on-Trent*

158　The lost piece of silver. The colouring of the glazes is green, light brown and yellow. Attributed to the younger Ralph Wood. Height 8¾″. *City Museum, Stoke-on-Trent*

159　Shepherd, decorated in coloured glazes. From the Wood factory. Height 8¾″. *Fitzwilliam Museum*

160　Shepherdess, pair to the figure on the left. Height 8¾″. *Fitzwilliam Museum*

157 158

159 160

89

161 Rustic group. The coloured glazes used are brown, green, blue, a pale straw colour and black. Made by the Woods before 1785. Height 9½″. *City Museum, Stoke-on-Trent*

162 Stag in a light greyish brown on a green base. Probably made by the Woods before 1785. Height 8½″. *Fitzwilliam Museum*

163 Doe, pair to the stag on the left. Height 4½″.

164 Teapot in the form of an elephant attributed to the Woods. Covered with a manganese mottled glaze. Height 6½″. *c.* 1770–80.

162

163

164

165

166

167

165 Backview of a figure of Charity, showing the signature. Glazed with a colourless glaze. Made by R. Wood. *c.* 1760–70. Height 8¾″.

166 Fair Hebe jug, modelled by John Voyez and signed by him with the date 1788. Decorated in coloured glazes and made by R. M. Astbury (impressed on the base). 9½″ high. *V & A Museum*

167 Two figures of children symbolizing Autumn and Winter. Obviously from the Wood factory, but unmarked. *c.* 1770. Height 4″. *City Museum, Stoke-on-Trent*

168

169

170

168 Toby jug attributed to the younger Ralph Wood. *c.* 1770–80. Height 11½″. *V & A Museum*

169 Toby jug marked Ra Wood Burslem. *c.* 1770. Height 9¾″. *Sotheby and Co*

170 Four Toby jugs, all attributed to the younger Ralph Wood, except for the one on the right. They are all decorated in coloured glazes. From extreme left: Admiral Lord Howe; The Squire; a sailor sitting on a brass-bound chest. Heights 9¼″–11⅞″. *c.* 1760–80. *Sotheby.*

171

172

171 Cauliflower ware teapot. Josiah Wedgwood invented a particularly beautiful rich dark green glaze, which he used on ware of this type. An example of his early work, when he first started up on his own. *c*. 1760. Height $4\frac{1}{2}''$.

172 Canal side view of the Etruria works. Opened by the first Josiah Wedgwood in 1769 on 13 June (now demolished). *Wedgwood*

8 Josiah Wedgwood 1730-95

The Wedgwoods had long been established as potters in Staffordshire by the time young Josiah, the youngest of a large family, was born in 1730. He was nine when his father died and he went to work at once with his brother Thomas, to whom he was later apprenticed in 1744. Ten years later he was working with Thomas Whieldon, who encouraged him to make experiments. Five years later, he started up on his own account, in premises known as the Ivy House and Pot Works in Burslem, which he rented from two of his uncles for £10 a year.

When he was an apprentice he had contracted small pox which left him the physical handicap of a weak leg (which he later had to have amputated). Josiah Wedgwood worked tirelessly reorganizing factory operations as well as continuing with his experiments with different kinds of clay mixtures and glazes.

By about 1760, the dark mottled tortoiseshell ware that Whieldon and many other potters had been making, was going out of fashion, and by 1763, Wedgwood had perfected his cream-coloured earthenware, which was composed of ground flint and pipeclay and glazed with a silky lead glaze. This body finally superseded both delft and salt-glazed stoneware, in England as well as on the continent.

Neo-classicism was in the air, and this cream-coloured earthenware was made into classical shapes inspired by the discoveries at Pompeii and Herculaneum. Much of the tableware was left undecorated, some was painted with delightful borders based on geometric or floral shapes, and some was sent to Liverpool to be decorated by a new process of transfer printing by the firm of Sadler and Green.

In Moss's *Liverpool Guide* published in 1790, it is written that 'Copper-plate printing upon china and earthenware originated here in 1752 and remained a sometime secret with the inventors Messrs Sadler and Green'. (Who used it largely to decorate tiles.) By 1763 this firm was sending regular weekly accounts to Wedgwood for all the transfer printing that they were doing for him.

In 1765, Josiah Wedgwood was commissioned to make a tea service for Queen Charlotte. She was so impressed with the result that she appointed him 'Potter to the Queen' and gave him permission to call the cream-coloured earthenware 'Queensware' (a name that was to become a household word, and is still used by the firm of Wedgwood today).

In 1767 Josiah Wedgwood went into partnership with Thomas Bentley, the actual deed being signed in 1769, the same summer that saw the opening of Etruria, the new factory for the manufacture of ornamental wares.

Bentley was a likeable, modest, quiet man with an excellent head for business, and he remained on terms of intimate friendship with Wedgwood until his early death in 1780. He was only 50. Bentley looked after the London showrooms, supervised the decorating done at the Chelsea studios and relieved Wedgwood of many business worries.

After perfecting the body for his Queensware, he turned his attention to 'Egyptian black', or black basalt ware. This was made from the native clay and ground ironstone with the addition of ochre and oxide of manganese. This resulted in a fine hard stoneware that could be polished on a lapidary wheel. In this ware he made many busts, medallions and vases as well as tea services. The ware was sometimes decorated in the Etruscan style with red and white encaustic colours. Wedgwood said of the ware: 'The black is sterling and will last for ever.' (For other manufacturers of black basalt, please turn to the end of the chapter).

But the ware for which Wedgwood is best known is the dense vitrified stoneware ornamented with white figures on a coloured ground, that he called jasper ware. In fact 'Wedgwood' has become synonymous with blue-and-white jasper. He began experimenting with this ware about 1774 but it was not until about 1780 that the finest jasper was produced. Although he had tried to keep it a secret, the ware was soon imitated by many other potters, sometimes well, but sometimes with very indifferent results. In particular he distrusted Ralph Wedgwood the son of his cousin Thomas (see the letter written to Tom Byerley December 12 1790).★

Wedgwood employed many famous artists, including John Voyez, Flaxman, Stubbs and Hackwood to design the classical reliefs with which the wares were decorated. Lady Templetown designed some of the smaller medallions used for buckles and brooches, as well as a tea service. Although blue and white was the most popular colour combination, other colours were also used including a pretty, soft sage green, a bamboo yellow, lilac and black. The white relief ornaments were cast in little metal or alabaster moulds and sprigged on to the coloured body of the ware. The inspiration for jasper came from Imperial Roman cameo glass. His most famous piece was the Portland Vase (see page 103). To begin with Josiah Wedgwood did not mark his ware, but this practise was begun in 1771 and by 1772 most pieces carried an impressed stamp. This was very necessary because many other potters were copying his wares and Wedgwood was jealous of his reputation.

Wedgwood also made seals both in intaglio and cameo and vases in imitation of agate or porphyry. The largest creamware dinner service he ever made was for the Empress Catherine of Russia, it comprised over nine hundred pieces.

Just before Bentley's death in 1780, he introduced a whiter bodied ware, which he called 'Pearl White'. He wrote to Bentley about this in August 1779:

'Your idea of cream-colour having the merit of an original and the pearl white being considered as an imitation of some of the blue and white fabriques, either earthenware or porcelain, is perfectly right, and I should not hesitate a moment in preferring the former if I consulted my own taste and sentiments: but you know what Lady Dartmouth told us, that she and her friends were tired of cream colour, and so they would be of Angels, if they were shown for sale in every chandlers shop through the town. The pearl white must be considered a change rather than an improvement, and I must have something ready to succeed it when the public eye is palled. . .'★

★*Selected letters of Josiah Wedgwood* Edited: Finer and Savage: 1965 Cory Adams and Mackay Ltd.

173

174

175

173 Thomas Bentley, Wedgwood's partner from 1769–80. From a medallion modelled by Joachim Smith in 1774. *Wedgwood*

174 Josiah Wedgwood. From a medallion modelled by William Hackwood in 1777. *Wedgwood*

175 Painting by George Stubbs RA of the Wedgwood family in the grounds of Etruria Hall in 1780. A black basalt vase similar to the one on page 100 stands on a table by Josiah Wedgwood. *Wedgwood*

176 A dish from the Empress Catherine of Russia's table service for her palace of *La Grenouillière*. The full service consisted of 952 pieces. It was completed in 1774. Length 19½". *Victoria and Albert Museum*

Apart from table ware and decorative pieces, Wedgwood was also interested in ceramics for industrial purposes, and after much careful experiment he produced a very hard, dense stoneware which was used for pestles and mortars.

Josiah Wedgwood died in 1795 and was succeeded in the business not by his eldest son, but by his third son Josiah II. In addition to all the experiments in the actual making of pottery, Josiah Wedgwood had been instrumental in getting the roads improved and canals built. He introduced steam power and transformed the Staffordshire pottery manufactory from a semi-rural craft into a well-organized mass-production industry with a large distribution and export service.★

★Writing to Lord Auckland in 1792 about the relative state of the potteries in 1792 and 80 years before, he said that the worth of the annual output had increased from £10,000 to between £200,000 and £300,000.

Other manufacturers of black basalt
Richard Barker Lane End 1784–1808. Peter Barker of Mexborough Pottery *c.* 1804. E. J. Birch of Shelton 1796–1814. Leeds Pottery 1795–1815. Keeley and Toft, Hanley *c.* 1790. S. Hollins 1790–1800. Herculaneum, Liverpool *c.* 1810. S. Greenwood 1780–90. J. Neale 1778–86. E. Mayer, Hanley 1800–20. J. Glass, Hanley 1822–30. H. Palmer and J. Voyez 1769. Enoch Wood and Wood and Caldwell 1790–1818. Etruscan ware was also made at Swansea.

Other makers of jasper ware
B. Adams *c.* 1800–10. D. Steel, Burslem 1796–1824. Turner (Lane End) who made it as well as Wedgwood. Neale and Co 1778. Enoch Wood *c.* 1800 and James Dudson in the 1880's.

177

177 Cream-coloured earthenware dish, printed in black in Liverpool by Sadler and Green. Marked WEDGWOOD impressed. Made *c.* 1775. Length 18½″. *Victoria and Albert Museum*

178 Three vases with covers. Left: Porphyry ware, marked WEDGWOOD & BENTLEY 1772. Height 14″. Centre: Sprinkled Porphyry vase, marked WEDGWOOD 1783. Height 9½″. Right: Vase with surface marbling, 1783. Height 16″. *Wedgwood*

178

179

180

179 Pair of black basalt vases with applied cameo subjects. The reversible covers were made to convert to candle holders. Marked WEDGWOOD & BENTLEY. Made in 1775. Height 11″. *Wedgwood*

180 A tea-service in blue and white jasper ware. The designs called 'Domestic Employment' were drawn by Lady Templetown and modelled by William Hackwood. 1784. Height of teapot 4″. *Wedgwood*

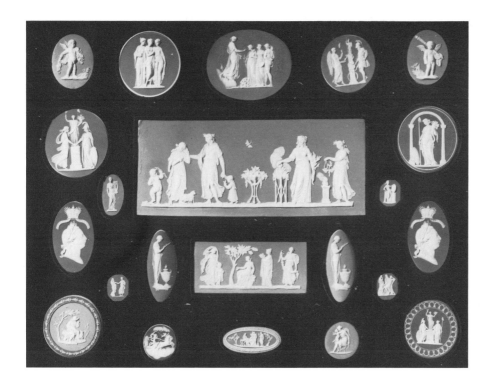

181 A collection of jasper ware medallions and plaques, made at Etruria between the years 1775–90. 'Sacrifice to Peace' in the centre. *Wedgwood*

182 Tripod vase in white and blue jasper. 1789. Height 8″. *Wedgwood*

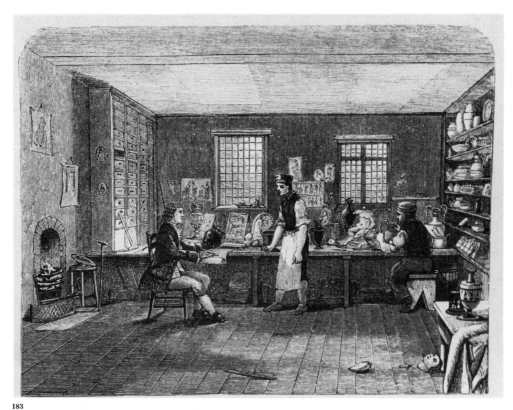

183
184

183 The modelling room at Etruria as it was in the early 1790's. Josiah Wedgwood discusses a vase with one of his modellers. *Wedgwood*

184 Etruscan vase. Black basalt with encaustic paintings in the Etruscan style. *c.* 1770. Height $13\frac{7}{8}''$. *Victoria and Albert Museum*

185 The Portland Vase. Josiah Wedgwood's copy, in black jasper with applied white figures, of the Greek vase brought to Italy in classical times and in the possession of the Barberini family at least from the 17th century. It was bought by the wife of the second Duke of Portland about 1780 and was lent to Wedgwood to copy in 1786. 13 numbered copies are known today and 7 unnumbered. Height $10\frac{1}{2}''$. *Wedgwood*

185

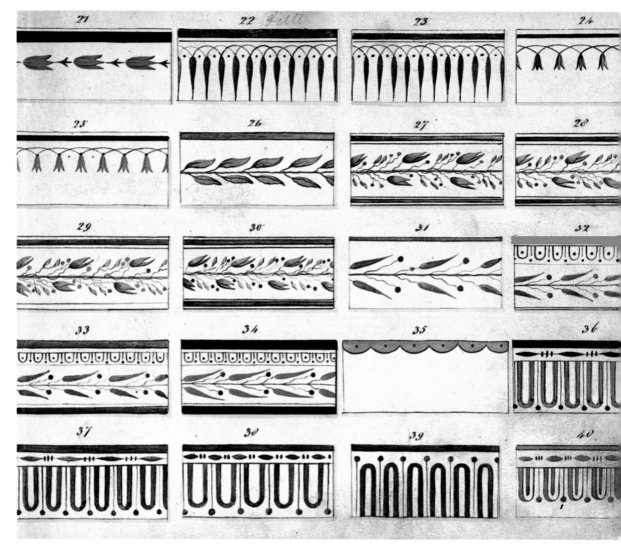

186 A page from one of the early Wedgwood pattern books, showing some of the border patterns used on Queensware. *Wedgwood*

9 Cream-coloured earthenware

Although Josiah Wedgwood was the first potter to produce cream-coloured earthenware on a commercial scale, other potters were quick to copy him. It was made by many other potters in Staffordshire, including the Turners of Lane End, who, surprisingly enough shipped much of their ware over to Holland to be decorated at Delft. Enoch Wood (the younger Ralph Wood's cousin) modelled a plaque of the family arms in cream-coloured earthenware when he was only eleven years old.

An excellent cream-coloured earthenware was made in Leeds, possibly from as early as 1765. The earliest of the Leeds cream ware is of a deep cream colour, very light and silky to the touch. By 1775, it was lighter in colour. A characteristic of the early ware was the use of double twisted or rope handle, ending where the handle joined the body with an embossed leafy terminal. A double reeded flat handle with floral or leafy terminals was used after about 1775. A curious knob, made in the form of a double convolvulus seems to be confined to the Leeds Pottery.

Very elaborate pieces were made in Leeds, with intricate piercing incorporated in the design. Some of these were *épergnes* or centre pieces about two feet high. Transfer printing in red, black and a purplish colour was used at Leeds, but not so well or so extensively as in Liverpool. The enamel coloured painting in a brick red and black was very typical of Leeds pottery though other colours were used also in designs adapted from oriental originals as well as from more traditionally English floral forms. Some of the ware was most effectively decorated simply in underglaze green stripes.

Although most of the production of the Leeds Pottery was useful ware, figures were also made similar in subjects to those made in Staffordshire. These are referred to on page 131.

Cream-coloured earthenware was certainly made in Liverpool before 1773, for a notice appears in *The Liverpool Advertiser* for 29 October 1773 advertising a pottery for sale on the south side of the town of Liverpool, including a large assortment of cream-coloured earthenwares. The Herculaneum Pottery, famous for its cream-coloured earthenware was established in the early 1790's by Richard Abbey. In 1796, over forty pottery workers from Staffordshire went to work there. The Liverpool cream-coloured earthenware was not so warm in colour as Wedgwood's Queensware.

Much of the ware was made for the American market and is transfer-printed with subjects to suit the American taste, the national Eagle, native scenes and ships. Jugs and punch bowls were made in large quantities. The Herculaneum factory closed down in 1841.

At Swansea a factory was started in the mid 1760's and cream-coloured earthenware was produced there that very much resembled that made by Wedgwood, though the earlier productions of the factory were glazed with a softish glaze that was apt to scratch, sometimes the glaze is so thin that it is almost like a salt glaze. The earlier body used at Swansea is perhaps a little unrefined, but some of the later ware is of very good quality. It is not so light in weight as the Leeds cream-coloured earthenware.

Though some transfer-printed ware was made here, the best known of the Swansea cream ware were some beautifully painted plates with flowers after the style of the hand-coloured engravings in Curtis's *Botanical Magazine*. These were done by Evan Evans, Thomas Pardoe and William Young. There was also a set of plates decorated with birds based on the illustrations in *British Birds* by Thomas Bewick, which first came out in 1797.

187 Plaque of the Wood arms, modelled in cream-coloured earthenware by Enoch Wood at the age of 11, in 1771. 9½″ square. *Wood and Sons Limited*

188 Plaque modelled in cream-coloured earthenware. Made in Staffordshire. *c.* 1780. Height 11⅜″. *Willett Collection, Brighton*

189 Night lamps and food warmers, late eighteenth century. Made in Leeds or Staffordshire. The smaller one is 9⅞″ high. *Victoria and Albert Museum*

190 Sauce boat and ladle. Made in Leeds. *c.* 1775. Height 5½″. *Victoria and Albert Museum*

187

188

189
190

191

192

193

194

195

196

197

198

191 Chestnut basket, with intricate pierced decoration. Made in Leeds. Marked HARTLEY GREENS & CO LEEDS POTTERY. *c.* 1780. Height 11″. *Temple Newsam, Leeds*

192 Leech jar with pierced cover. Early nineteenth century, made in Staffordshire or Leeds. Every apothecaries' shop would have had its leech jar at that time. The use of leeches now is said to be confined to actors who happen to have black eyes. Height 11¼″. *Pharmaceutical Society*

193 Coffee pot with reeded twisted double handle. Leeds or Staffordshire. *c.* 1790. Height 12″. *Victoria and Albert Museum*

194 Coffee pot transfer printed in black. Made in Leeds. *c.* 1800. Height 10½″. *Victoria and Albert Museum*

195 Teapot with portrait of King George III and double twisted handle. Made in Leeds in the 1760's. Height 5″. *City Museum, Stoke-on-Trent*

196 Teapot and cover, printed in black with a transfer design 'The Tea-party'. Probably Wedgwood. *c.* 1763. Height 5″. *City Museum, Stoke-on-Trent*

197 Teapot decorated with underglaze green stripes, with double twisted handle with floral terminals. Made in Leeds about 1780. Height 5½″. *Victoria and Albert Museum*

198 Teapot with hand painted floral decoration in red, green, purple and black; double twisted handle. Made in Leeds. *c.* 1780. Height 5¾″.

Cup love and friendship,
Peace and good neighbourhood
May we never see an ould friend,
With a new face

199

Henry Muns
Northamptonshire

200

EAST VIEW OF THE
MANUFACTORIES
OF
ENOCH WOOD & SONS
BURSLEM

201

202   203

199 Loving-cup, painted in enamel colours. Made in Leeds. *c.* 1775. Height 7½". *Temple Newsam, Leeds*

200 Jug decorated with emblems of the sweep's trade. Made in Staffordshire. *c.* 1800. Height 10¼". *Willett Collection, Brighton*

201 This jug was presented to Joseph Bailey by Joseph Wood 'for the great attention and humanity rendered to him after his providential escape from the wreck of the Earl Moira on the 9 August 1821' Joseph Wood (born 1795) was the brother of Enoch Wood II. *The Earl of Moira* was the Liverpool–Dublin packet; she went down on the Burbo Bank near Liverpool with the loss of forty lives. She was a cutter of 89 tons and built in 1808. This jug must have been made at Enoch Wood's factory in 1821. There are two views of the factory on the sides of the jug and the inscription under the spout. Transfer printed in black with hand painted lettering. Height 14¼". *Wood and Sons Limited.*

202 Wedgwood Queensware plate, transfer printed in red, the illustration 'The Tiger and the Fox', coming from *Aesop's Fables. c.* 1775. 10" dia. Marked WEDGWOOD. *Victoria and Albert Museum*

203 Cream-coloured earthenware plate with identical border to the previous plate. This one is unmarked. There are however identically bordered plates marked LEEDS POTTERY that were made *c.* 1780. The ship is a collier brig and from her general appearance, would give the impression of belonging to the nineteenth rather than the eighteenth century. Dia. 9¾". *Collection : Hugh Green*

204

204 Supper dish in cream-coloured earthenware marked WEDGWOOD impressed. The vine border is hand painted. *c*. 1790. Dia. 20″. *Victoria and Albert Museum*

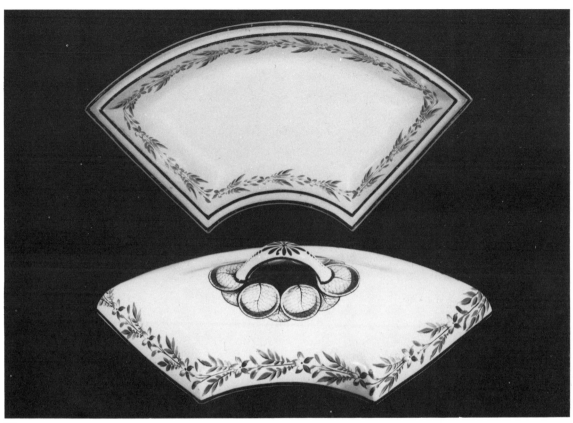

205

205 A quarter of a supper dish with its cover made in cream-coloured earthenware, painted in green and grey with a border of white jasmine, manganese design round the handle and edging borders. Marked SWANSEA impressed. The glaze is softer and more easily scratched than the Wedgwood Queensware. *c.* 1780. $13\frac{1}{4}''$ across.

206　　　　　　　　　　　　　　207

206　Black transfer printed tile signed by J. Sadler and made in Liverpool. *c.* 1765. 5″ sq. *Fitzwilliam Museum*

207　Red transfer printed tile by Sadler and Green of Liverpool. *c.* 1775. 5″ sq. *Fitzwilliam Museum*

208　Cream-coloured earthenware jug, with a black transfer decoration, from a drawing by Hogarth of a cock fight. Made in Liverpool. *c.* 1780. Height 9½″. *Victoria and Albert Museum*

209　Cream-coloured earthenware jug commemorating the fall of the Bastille. Black transfer print, probably by Sadler and Green. Made in Liverpool. *c.* 1790. Height 7½″.
　　　The Liverpool cream-coloured earthenware was paler and greyer in colour than that made in Staffordshire or Leeds. *Victoria and Albert Museum*

208　　　　　　　　　　　　　　209

210

211

212

213

210 Dessert plate of cream coloured earthenware painted with a bladder hibiscus. Marked Swansea and a spade impressed. *c.* 1800–10. Dia. $8\frac{1}{8}''$. *Victoria and Albert Museum*

211 Dessert dish painted with a striped carnation. Marked SWANSEA and an impressed spade mark. *c.* 1800–10. Dia. 8″. *Victoria and Albert Museum*

212 Dinner plate with a shell edge and painted with armorial bearings. Swansea. Early nineteenth century. Dia. 8″. *Victoria and Albert Museum*

213 Swansea plate decorated with a black transfer print of a merchant brig of about 1800. Marked DILLWYN impressed. The artist has drawn the pre-Union Jack. *c.* 1801–1817. Dia. $8\frac{7}{8}''$.

115

214

215

216

217

214 Pratt ware jug modelled in relief with scenes of the Sailor's Return and Farewell and formalized acanthus borders. The colouring of all these jugs is similar, the browns, yellows, blues, greens and black of oxide colours under the glaze. This jug is marked PRATT impressed underneath. *c.* 1790–1800. Height $6\frac{1}{8}''$.

215 A similar jug with Britannia on one side and the Sailor's Return on the other. Marked PRATT impressed. Height 5″.

216 A similar jug moulded in relief with bucolic scenes. Marked WEDGWOOD impressed. Height $6\frac{1}{4}''$. *c.* 1800.

217 A similar jug with Admiral Duncan on one side and Captain Trollope on the other. *c.* 1797. Marked W.DANIEL impressed. Height $7\frac{3}{4}''$. This jug is of a creamier and grittier body than the others.

116

10 Pratt ware c. 1790-1830

UNDERGLAZE COLOURED EARTHENWARE AND FIGURES

Pratt ware is the generic name for the particularly attractive underglaze coloured earthenware made from about 1790–1830. The ware is most widely known for the jugs with designs moulded in relief of sporting and bucolic scenes or commemorative subjects, including naval and military heroes.

The body of the ware was usually white, but sometimes of a pale cream colour, the lead glaze was sometimes slightly tinged with blue. The colours used were limited to the oxide colours that could withstand the heat necessary to fuse the glaze; blue, yellows, oranges, greens, browns and black. (A typical maiolica palette in fact.)

Other objects besides jugs were made including plaques, tea caddies, flasks, teapots, mugs, dishes, vases, cornucopiae, watchstands, candlesticks and figures.

Pratt ware varies very much in the quality of the ware itself, and also of the painted decoration. The quality of the modelling varies of course too, depending on the condition of the moulds. Old worn moulds give a blurred impression.

Those made by Pratt himself were not necessarily the best; though he was said to have considered himself a better potter than Josiah Wedgwood. He was working in Fenton from 1775–1810, and although a few jugs have been found with his impressed mark, they are extremely uncommon.

Though the majority of Pratt jugs are unmarked, there are jugs and other pieces of Pratt-type ware marked with the names of other makers. These include: WEDGWOOD, BARKER, HARLEY, HAWLEY, DIXON AUSTIN & CO, E. BOURNE, WOOD, W. DANIEL, LEEDS POTTERY, FERRYBRIDGE, ASTBURY, NEWCASTLE, JACOB MARSH and a mysterious, unidentified, large impressed crown mark.

WEDGWOOD is more likely to be the mark of Ralph Wedgwood (a somewhat peripatetic potter and cousin of Josiah's) than Josiah himself. Ralph was working in Burslem 1785–96 and then later on went to Ferrybridge.

BARKER was a well-known potting family in Staffordshire; John, William and Richard Barker are listed as makers of cream-coloured earthenware in 1786 and Richard Barker was again in the 1802 list. There were Barkers potting at Rawmarsh near Rotherham in Yorkshire before 1800 and in Mexborough after 1804.

HARLEY was the mark of a potter called Thomas Harley who was working at Lane End in Staffordshire c. 1802–8. He made curious diamond-shaped teapots with moulded borders of stiff leaves very much in the Pratt style. However, his painted decoration on these varied from pseudo-Chinese landscapes to rather clumsily drawn wide blue lines edging the moulded borders, combined with a few sparse gilt and blue painted flowers.

HAWLEY was a potter working in Staffordshire or Yorkshire at the beginning of the nineteenth century. O. Grabham (*Yorkshire Potteries, Pots and Potters*: 1916) says William Hawley established the Top Pottery at Rawmarsh in 1790.

DIXON, AUSTIN & CO ran the Garrison Pottery at Sunderland from 1820–26.

E. BOURNE started a pottery in Staffordshire sometime after 1773 (it was later taken over by the great firm of Davenport).

W. DANIEL is in the Burslem list of earthenware makers in 1786 and in 1802.

WOOD was possibly John Wood, who was making cream-coloured earthenware from 1782 until he was murdered in 1797. Or it was perhaps Enoch Wood, who certainly produced ware of a very good quality, but who marked his things E. Wood or Enoch Wood, later Wood and Caldwell and later still Enoch Wood and Sons. However, it is thought possible that he used the name WOOD occasionally.

ASTBURY was probably R. M. Astbury who carried on with the Foley works after the retirement of his father Joshua Astbury. He produced very good work, but went bankrupt in 1797. The Voyez 'Fair Hebe' jug in underglaze colouring is sometimes marked R. M. Astbury.

NEWCASTLE: this mark is usually pencilled with a cursive hand. There were several small potteries in Newcastle-upon-Tyne in the early nineteenth century. (There is a very crude plaque so marked in the Victoria and Albert Museum).

LEEDS POTTERY made cream coloured earthenware from c. 1775–1800. Their Pratt-type jugs are made in this ware, usually featuring Lord Nelson and Captain Berry.

FERRYBRIDGE: the pottery not far from Leeds where Ralph Wedgwood worked from 1796–1800. While he was there, they used the mark Wedgwood and Co, and they used the FERRYBRIDGE mark after 1804.

Many underglaze coloured figures were made, ranging from simple little figures of children haphazardly spotted with different colours, to quite large figures, Toby jugs and animals, including large bull-baiting groups.

Many underglaze coloured figures were taken from the same moulds as the earlier coloured-glaze figures of Whieldon and the Woods. Because of the colouring, today they all tend to be grouped under the one heading of 'Pratt', but they were certainly made in as many districts as the rest of the so-called Pratt ware. It is very rare to find marked figures.

There are sets of *The Seasons*, in underglaze colouring taken obviously from the Ralph Wood *Seasons*, that were made at the Garrison Pottery at Sunderland from 1820–26. These are occasionally found marked DIXON, AUSTIN & CO; similar figures are found marked LEEDS POTTERY. (See page 131). The Leeds figures are lighter in weight and of a creamier colour than the Sunderland figures.

Toby and Bacchus jugs (the latter originally designed by John Voyez) were also made in underglaze colouring. Some of the Toby jugs are marked with a large impressed crown, and there are some disproportionately large sheep with small attendant figures made at the same elusive pottery that used this crown mark.

Jacob Marsh (whose pottery is located on the 1800 map of Burslem) made charming little figures, modelled very much in the Wood manner (see page 121). He sometimes marked his figures with his name pencilled in blue under the base in a rather rustic cursive hand. He appears in Parson and Bradshaws Directory in 1818 among the Lane End potters.

Until comparatively recently the underglaze figures were somewhat neglected; in the salerooms they now fetch the sort of prices that Ralph Wood figures with coloured glazes were fetching before the war.

218

219

220

221

218 A similar jug depicting Admiral Jervis, made soon after the battle of Cape St Vincent in 1797. Unmarked. Height 6″.

219 A similar jug, the design showing a medallion each side with Mischievous Sport and Sportive Innocence impressed. Very similar to a Castleford type of stoneware jug, illustrated on page 72. This one is unmarked. c. 1800. Height 6″.

220 A similar jug with portraits of Admiral Nelson and Captain Berry. c. 1797. Marked LEEDS POTTERY. Height 6¼″. A creamier colour than most of the jugs of the Pratt type.

221 A similar jug showing Lord Nelson with his amputated arm, probably made soon after the incident, which happened at Santa Cruz in 1797. Unmarked. Height 5⅛″.

222 A teapot with moulded decoration and painted with a landscape on each side in underglaze colours. Marked BARKER impressed. Made in Yorkshire or Staffordshire. *c.* 1790–1800. Height 6½″.

223 A teapot with moulded decoration painted in underglaze colouring. Marked ASTBURY impressed. Probably R.M. Astbury. *c.* 1795. Height 5⅜″.

224

225

224 Three small figures decorated in underglaze colouring. They bear a resemblance to some of the early Wood figures. The child with the basket of fishes is marked in cursive blue lettering under the base Jacob Marsh. Made in Staffordshire at the beginning of the nineteenth century. Height of largest figure 6½".

225 Five small moulded figures, decorated somewhat haphazardly with dabs of colour under the glaze. Made in Staffordshire during the last quarter of the eighteenth century. The one on the extreme right is very light in weight and may be a little earlier. None of them is marked. Average height 4½"–5".

Photo: Bob Alcock

226 Pratt jug of a rather unusual shape. Moulded and painted in blue, greens, yellow and orange and brown. The borders round the medallions on the sides have been sprigged on, which is also unusual. The pictorial subject is a common one, the Sailor's Return and Farewell. *c.* 1800. Height 7″.

227　　　　　　　　**228**

229

227 Toby jug obviously made at the same factory as the group of figures below. Note the treatment of eyebrows, bases and the model of the dog. Marked on the base with a large impressed crown. At the moment the pottery has not been identified. *c.* 1790–1800. Height 9¾″. *Collection: Hugh Radcliffe-Wilson*

228 Fern pot marked E. BOURNE impressed. Made in Staffordshire. *c.* 1790–1800. 6″ high. *Manheim Collection*

229 Two watchstands and a gigantic sheep, obviously from the same pottery as the Toby jug above. *c.* 1800–1810. Height of watchstands 8½″.

123

230

231

232

230 Plaque moulded in relief and decorated with underglaze colours. A portrait of the actress Sarah Siddons (1755–1831). *c.* 1790. Height 8½″. *Willett Collection, Brighton*

231 Plaque decorated with relief modelling and underglaze colouring. Attributed to Ralph Wood junior. *c.* 1770. 10¼″ high. *City Museum, Stoke-on-Trent*

232 A set of the Seasons, after Ralph Wood models. Decorated in underglaze colouring. The same figures also occur with pink lustre decoration, and similar figures are found mounted on high square bases ornamented with stiff leaves (as on figure 233). Marked DIXON, AUSTIN & CO. Made in Sunderland. *c.* 1820–26. Height of tallest 10¼″.

233 234
235 236

233 Figure of Hope, rather crudely modelled and striped in yellow and brown. Figures on this type of base have been attributed to Liverpool. This one however is rather creamy in colour, and looks more like the work of some Staffordshire potter. c. 1800. Height 8¼".

234 A horse and a foot volunteer. Have been variously attributed to Newcastle, Portobello, Staffordshire and some Yorkshire potteries. c. 1790–1800. Height 9". *Willett Collection, Brighton*

235 Figure of a drunken Irishman riding on a pig. Made in Staffordshire. c. 1890. The base is decorated with threads of clay in imitation of straw. Height 6¾". *Willett Collection, Brighton*

236 Group of horse, thrown rider and dog sponged with light olive green and grey and yellow under the glaze. Made in Staffordshire. c. 1780. Height 8". *Willett Collection, Brighton*

237

238

239

126

240

237 A boy and girl watching two cocks fighting, decorated in pale underglaze yellows, blues and grey-greens. Made in Staffordshire. *c.* 1790. Height 8″. *Willett Collection, Brighton*

238 Giant shepherdess with diminutive sheep. Decorated with particularly good underglaze colours, mainly blue, yellow and green. *c.* 1790. Height 8″. *Fitzwilliam Museum*

239 A particularly delightful figure of a lion decorated with strong underglaze orange, blue and black. Made in Staffordshire. *c.* 1790. Height 5½″. *City Museum, Stoke-on-Trent*

240 A transitional figure decorated in a combination of underglaze and enamel colours over the glaze. Known as the 'Hearty Good Fellow'. He is holding a miniature Pratt jug in his hand. Made in Staffordshire. *c.* 1790. Height 12″.

241

242

241, 242, 243
Three large pearlware figures of horses. No 241 is decorated with enamel
colours and the other two are spotted or sponged with colours under the
glaze. Made for display in the windows of harness makers and corn
chandlers, horse doctors and chemists specializing in veterinary supplies.
Made at the Leeds Pottery between 1800–1820. Height 16″. *Temple
Newsam and Sotheby & Co*

11 Pearl ware

The 'Pearl white' ware that Wedgwood had developed in the late 1770's as a successor to his cream-coloured earthenware was taken up by other potters, though it never achieved the same popularity that the earlier ware had done. It was soon eclipsed by the kind of ware made by Spode and his followers, which was a very pale cream or even white, without the slightest tinge of the grey that is characteristic of pearl ware.

Apart from the jugs and other useful ware, the pearl ware body was used for the manufacture of figures. This was especially so at Leeds where a number of pearl ware figures were made. Some of the most delightful of these were models of horses (they were also made in cream-coloured earthenware), some 15–16" high. These large models were something of a technical triumph for the earthenware potters, for the legs were thin and delicate and quite unsupported.

These horses were finished in a variety of ways; some were painted in enamel colours, others were spotted or dappled with underglaze colours. They were bought by saddlers and chemists who specialized in veterinary supplies, for the decoration of their shops.

243

244

245

244 Set of the *Seasons* marked Neale and Co impressed. Made in Staffordshire. *c*. 1780. Height 5⅜″. On first sight, these figures are more like porcelain than earthenware. The enamel colours are very precisely painted. *Fitzwilliam Museum*

245 A group of three classical figures on square bases. On the left: Hygieia standing beside a flaming altar, water jug in one hand, serpent in the other. Marked with an impressed 'D'. Similar to a Wood figure of the later period. *c*. 1790. Height 9½″. The centre figure Charity is stamped with the WEDGWOOD mark. *c*. 1800. 8¾″ high. On the right, Andromache in a pink robe with crimson flowers. Probably Ralph Wood the younger or Enoch Wood. *c*. 1790. Height 9¼″. *Fitzwilliam Museum*

12 Enamel coloured figures

Towards the end of the eighteenth century, the coloured glaze figures and the underglaze coloured figures were followed by figures decorated with enamel colours. These colours were painted on after the piece had been glazed and then the figure was re-fired at a much lower temperature to fix the enamels. This meant that a very much wider range of colours could be used.

Two of the first potters to take advantage of this new technique were Ralph Wood the younger (1748–95) and his cousin Enoch Wood. Ralph Wood continued to produce some of the figures that his father had made, but instead of the coloured glazes, he used these enamel colours; he made other figures very much in the same style of modelling as that used by his father. Some of these he marked 'Ra Wood.' These new models included busts of Milton, Shakespeare and other personages both respectable and famous. Ralph Wood the younger died before he was fifty.

Enoch Wood (1759–1840) had begun modelling at a very early age (see the plaque on page 106). At the age of eighteen, he modelled a very complicated jasper ware plaque based on the Rubens' painting *The Descent from the Cross*. A little later he made busts of both Wesley and Whitfield and many other pieces of a pious nature, as well as some allegorical figures such as *Prudence* and *Fortitude*. *Charity* occurs with the Wedgwood mark.

After being apprenticed to Humphrey Palmer of Hanley, Enoch Wood had at first worked with his cousin Ralph and they both made enamel coloured figures and Toby jugs. They were well modelled and attractive in colouring. About 1790 he went into partnership with James Caldwell and the firm used the mark WOOD & CALDWELL. In 1819, he bought Caldwell out and took some of his own sons into partnership (he had twelve children) and the firm became Enoch Wood and Sons. He lived to be over eighty.

Enoch Wood had made a large and representative collection of pottery telling the story of the industry up to 1830. Unfortunately at his death this was broken up and dispersed. The catalogue, if one ever existed, was lost. Fully documented, such a collection would have been of inestimable value to future students and collectors.

Other early enamel coloured figure makers include James Neale (who took on Palmer's business in 1778) and Robert Wilson, who succeeded Neale. Lakin and Poole made good quality figures from about 1770–94 though marked examples are rare.

The Leeds Pottery made some creamware figures decorated in enamel colours, as well as pearlware figures. They date from about 1790–1800. It is a little difficult to generalize, but on the whole the Leeds figures are lighter in weight and are also slightly more naive than their Staffordshire counterparts. If they are mounted on square bases, these generally are a little higher than the Staffordshire ones.

Figures were made in Liverpool at the Herculaneum pottery, but as many of the employees of this pottery had migrated there from Staffordshire, the Liverpool figures are very similar to those made in Staffordshire, though again, marked examples are extremely rare.

A slightly different type of figure made its appearance about the beginning of the nineteenth century, inspired by the porcelain figures from the continent and from Chelsea and Bow. These consisted of a figure or a group of figures mounted on a green rocky base or a rococo scrolled mound and backed by an elaborate tree with formalized greenery and flowers. The name that occurs most frequently on this type of figure is that of John Walton, who signed his name in either impressed or embossed roman capitals on a scroll at the back of the base. The names of other potters including Ralph Salt and Charles Tittensor are sometimes found though most of this type of figure is unmarked. Dozens of potters were engaged on the production of these charming little figures, which they made by the hundred and sold very cheaply.

Potters were always going out of business and sales of potteries were frequently advertised in the newspapers, showing the whole stock-in-trade of a factory including moulds. This would account for the fact that it is quite possible to come across identical figures with entirely different painting. Obviously a well-finished and beautifully decorated piece would not have come from the same factory as a poorly finished specimen.

Many of Walton's figures are of religious subjects such as the *Widow of Zarephath* and *Elijah and the Raven*, as well as saints and apostles, though he also modelled classical goddesses and arcadian figures of shepherds and shepherdesses, gardeners and putti, lions and unicorns, sheep and rams with a bocage background. Walton's pottery was working from about 1815–35.

The Staffordshire potters also made cottages, churches and castles. These were sometimes purely ornamental, but others were made in the form of a money-box with a slit in the roof, or a pastille burner with an arched opening at the back and pierced windows.

Obadiah Sherratt, who is recorded as being a master potter of Burslem in 1822, made very distinctive figures or groups of figures. These had a crudeness and barbarity lacking in the prettier Walton type of figure. Bull baiting, cock and dog fighting were popular sports among the hard-working potters in the early years of the nineteenth century, when drunkenness was a common vice. Sherratt caricatured such things in his broad earthy groups, which have an attractive fairground quality in spite of the subject matter. His factory remained in production until the middle of the nineteenth century.

246 An enamel coloured bust of Shakespeare, by Enoch Wood and a bust of Milton by the younger Ralph Wood, glazed with a colourless glaze. Made *c.* 1790. Height 10″.

247 Figure of Diana decorated with enamel colours, made by Ralph Wood the younger. *c.* 1780–90. Height 11½″. John Walton made a later version of this figure. *Fitzwilliam Museum*

248 The Assassination of Marat. A group made by Lakin and Poole (marked). *c.* 1794. Height 13½″. *Fitzwilliam Museum*

246

247 248

The Assassination of MARAT.
by CHARLOTTE. CORDE.
of Caen, in Normandy.
1793

133

249

250

251

249 A group of shepherds and gardeners inspired by the porcelain figures of Chelsea or Meissen. All made by John Walton and marked WALTON impressed on a scroll behind the base. *c.* 1820. Height approx. 5″.

250 A charmingly naive rustic group made by John Walton (marked). *c.* 1815. Height 7″.

251 Rualers. An early nineteenth century group, inspired by an earlier Wood model (see page 90). After the style of John Walton but unmarked. The lettering is impressed from printers' types; an & has been used to substitute for an S. *c.* 1815. Height 6½″.

252

253

252 Three Staffordshire sheep. The two on the left are marked WALTON. The ram on the right is marked SALT. *c.* 1820. Height 7½″.

253 A group of putti made by different Staffordshire potters in the early years of the nineteenth century. The central figure is possibly by Neale, but none of them are marked. Height of tallest 7″.

254 A mounted general, attributed to Walton, but unmarked. *c.* 1815. Height 10¼". *Fitzwilliam Museum*

255 Three Staffordshire cottages, centre and left are pastille burners. *c.* 1830. Height 4¼".

256 Politos Menagerie. A large group made by Obadiah Sherratt in Burslem. *c.* 1830. Height 11". *City Museum, Stoke-on-Trent*

257 Figure of a lion, made by Wood and Caldwell; early nineteenth century. Height 9½". *City Museum, Stoke-on-Trent*

254
255

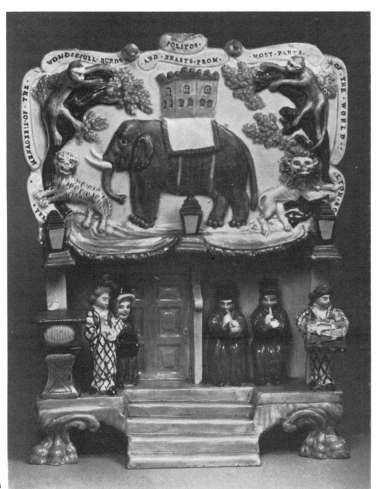

256

257

137

258

259

258 Bull-baiting group made in Staffordshire by Obadiah Sherratt. *c.* 1830. This type of stand was typical of the Sherratt figures. Height 11″. *Willett Collection, Brighton*

259 Lieutenant Monroe being carried off by a tiger. This gruesome occurance took place somewhere near Calcutta on 2 December 1792. This may have been one of Sherratt's earliest groups, but cannot have been as early as this. Possibly 1815. Height 9¾″.

138

Photo: John Webb

260 Venus with a cherub and a dolphin. Attributed to Obadiah Sherratt. This figure group also is found mounted on a similar stand to that used on illustrations 232 and 233. Impressed VENUS from printers type. *c.* 1820. Height 8″. *Victoria and Albert Museum*

261

262

263

261 Tee Total. A moral group by Obadiah Sherratt. *c.* 1820. Height 7¾″. *Willett Collection, Brighton*

262 Perswaition. Sometimes inscribed thus, and sometimes mounted on a Sherratt type stand. This is more in the Walton style generally. *c.* 1815–20, No mark. Height 8″. *Willett Collection, Brighton*

263 Mantlepiece ornament with a solemn warning in a fat faced type (*c.* 1808). Made in Staffordshire. *c.* 1820.

264

265

264 Pair of figures probably made by Sherratt, *c.* 1815–20. The Lady is 7¼″ high.

265 A pair of groups in an arbour setting. Staffordshire. *c.* 1820. Height 7″.

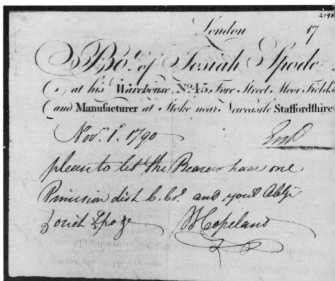

266 Miniature of Josiah Spode the first (1733–1797). Height 2⅜″. *Collection: R.R.J.Copeland* CBE, DL, JP

267 An engraved letterheading used at the Spode factory in the late eighteenth century. The signature is of W. Copeland who was closely associated with Josiah Spode the first, and whose son eventually became sole owner of the Spode factory in 1847. Hence the name W.T.Copeland & Sons in an unbroken succession to the present day. *W.T.Copeland Museum*

268 A double spread from the fourth of the old pattern books of Josiah Spode. The first of these books was begun in 1770. *W.T.Copeland Museum*

13 Josiah Spode and transfer printing

LATE EIGHTEENTH CENTURY UNDERGLAZE BLUE TRANSFER
PRINTING AND NINETEENTH CENTURY TRANSFER-PRINTED WARES

Before considering the pottery figures of the mid-nineteenth century, it is necessary to look back to the eighteenth century again, to see another influence at work.

The taste of Josiah Wedgwood had been influenced almost entirely by the Neo-classical movement. He was not particularly attracted by oriental art or influenced by the Chinese inspired designs then being painted in underglaze blue at the porcelain factories of Worcester and Caughley.

It was Josiah Spode (he had been apprenticed to Whieldon and was three years younger than Josiah Wedgwood) who in 1781, introduced underglaze blue transfer printing into Staffordshire. He employed two men from the Caughley factory, Thomas Lucas, an engraver, and James Richards, a printer. Spode no doubt saw (as Wedgwood had remarked in 1779) that the public was always demanding a change and the intricately engraved transfer-printed blue patterns in the oriental taste which he introduced to Staffordshire in 1781 were certainly a change from the plain or sparsely decorated Queensware of the preceding period. Mintons (Spode's great rivals) and many other Staffordshire potters as well as potters in other districts, were quick to follow Spode's lead and the production of blue transfer-printed earthenware continued throughout the nineteenth century. In fact until the present day, as versions of the famous 'Willow' pattern are still made by various firms including Ridgways. (See page 214).

From 1781–1833 literally dozens of patterns were engraved by the Spode engravers, and altogether, hundreds of designs must have been made by the English potters. Many were copied from Chinese designs, others from Indian and Italian originals (though on the whole very few of them were Neo-classical). A large series of designs were taken by the Spode factory from a book of engravings called: *Views in the Ottoman Empire chiefly in Caramania, a port of Asia Minor, hitherto unexplored with some curious selections from the Island of Rhodes and Cyprus, and the celebrated cities of Corinth, Carthage and Tripoli, from the original drawings in possession of Sir R. Ainslie, taken during his Embassy to Constantinople by Luigi Mayer.* This was published in 1803, but no mention is made of the name of the engraver. It became common practice for the potters to borrow their designs wholesale from books of this sort, and the whole surface of the ware was covered in the resulting prints.

The body of Spode's earthenware varied in colour from very pale cream to pure white and it had a silky-feeling glaze. It is very light in weight compared to modern earthenware.

Although the early blue-and-white transfer-printed ware was mainly bought by the professional classes, when mass production really got under way it became less and less expensive, until it was within the reach of everybody. A large export trade with America grew up, Enoch Wood's factory exporting ship loads of printed ware, much specially designed for that market. Other colours were also used on the transfer-printed tablewares of the nineteenth century. Many of the more expensive designs were transfer-printed in a basic outline of either grey or purple and enamel colours were filled in by hand on top of the glaze when it had been fired. Other transfers were printed in black or red.

A good white earthenware with transfer printed designs was made by W. Smith and Co of Stockton-on-Tees from about 1825–55. William Smith produced a good blue 'Willow' pattern which he marked 'Queensware'; other patterns printed in black like his 'Tourist' pattern (see page 147) he shamelessly stamped WEDGEWOOD (with an 'E' in the middle) until the Wedgwood firm prevented him from doing this in 1848, by taking out an injunction against him.

Black transfer printing of a cruder and very different kind, showing no oriental influence whatever, was done at various potteries in Sunderland: Dixon and Co, J. Phillips, Hylton Pottery, and Scott and Sons Southwick; though marked specimens are not common. The designs frequently included a view of the famous Iron Bridge over the river Wear that was opened in 1796; but many other subjects, particularly those with a nautical flavour are to be found. In addition to a picture, a verse was often included in the design and bands of pink lustre completed the decoration. Sometimes the whole background was covered in 'splashed' pink lustre. (See also section on lustre decoration, page 157).

Commemorative pieces were often produced both here and in Staffordshire; historical events, famous people and even the railways came in for their share of attention.

The body of the Sunderland ware (though the early specimens are light in weight) was usually rather heavy and thick and it was very white. It was obviously aimed at a popular market and was bought, to a very large extent, by the unsophisticated seafaring types that traded along the East coast.

Many different types of objects were manufactured, but the biggest trade of all must have been in bowls and jugs, mugs and basins. A macabre joke, copied from earlier ware, consisted of placing a large three dimensional frog or toad near the bottom of the mug, perhaps intended to have a sobering effect on hard drinkers.

Plaques were made inscribed with religious texts or lettered with solemn warnings 'Prepare to meet thy God' or 'The Eye of God sees't all'. These had also been made in Staffordshire, a wave of religious fervour sweeping through the country after the tour of John Wesley in 1781.

269 Pottery sections produced especially for the travellers, showing border decorations in full colour; all the patterns are free-hand painted and traced in various colours exactly as the finished plates. *W. T. Copeland Museum*

270 Small scale pottery model coloured under-glaze of the Spode factory as it was in about 1820. Each oven measures $2\frac{3}{4}''$ in height. Many of the parts of the model are recognisable with old buildings still left in the 1950's. *W. T. Copeland Museum*

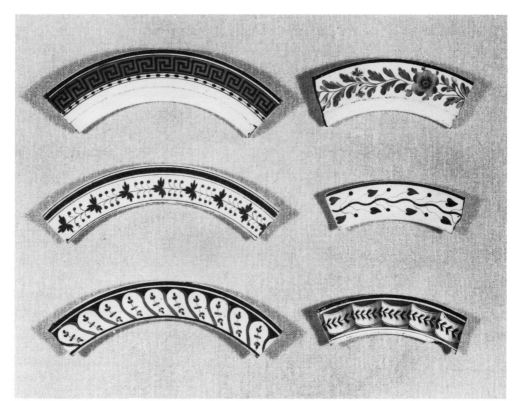

145

271

272

273

274

275   276

277

271 Earthenware plate: Caramanian pattern, printed in cobalt blue under the glaze. A very fine production where Spode used old prints as a basis for the centre decoration. The scene depicts 'Sarcophagi and Sepulchres at the head of the harbour at Cacamo'. The border of animals, figures etc. is not quite in keeping with the centre, and an attempt has been made by the artist to tie in the two by including palm trees in the centre, which do not appear in the original print. The engraving technique is mainly stipple and punch-work very finely executed. *c.* 1809. Dia. 10″. Impressed SPODE. *Collection: R.R.J.Copeland* CBE, DL, JP

272 Earthenware plate: Greek pattern printed in cobalt blue under the glaze. The quality of the engraving in this series is of the highest standard and much research must have been carried out to find sufficient subjects for all the different pieces in this very large service. *c.* 1820. Dia. 9¾″. *Collection: R.R.J.Copeland* CBE, DL, JP

273 Willow pattern plate transfer printed in under-glaze blue. Made by Dillwyn and Co, Swansea. *c.* 1820. Dia. 9½″. *Victoria and Albert Museum*

274 Earthenware plate: Floral pattern. Blue printed floral cartouche on the back with the word 'Floral' in script, also impressed SPODE in small capitals. Printed in cobalt blue under the glaze. A delightful pattern quite distinct in style from other Spode blue decorations. Practically the whole of this pattern is engraved using line work. Each piece has a different botanical floral centre and all are remarkably good. This pattern was one of the later productions of the Spode period and reflects great credit on the craftsmen of the time. In the centre of this plate is a passion flower. *c.* 1825. Dia. 10″. *W.T.Copeland Museum*

275 White earthenware plate, transfer printed in a rich dark blue under the glaze. Made by Enoch Wood and Sons (printed in blue on the back) specially for the American market. *c.* 1830. Dia. 10″. *Victoria and Albert Museum*

276 White earthenware drug jar, printed in underglaze blue. The border used is known as the 'Union Wreath' and came in shortly after the Union with Ireland in 1800. The electuary Mithridates was supposed to have been invented by King Mithridates of Pontus and Bythynia. It was composed of 54 ingredients and was supposed to be a powerful antidote against poison. The jar is impressed SPODE in blue. *c.* 1800. Height 7½″. *Pharmaceutical Society*

277 White deep earthenware dish. Transfer printed in black under the glaze. On the back a cartouche with the word 'Tourist' and W.S. & Co and impressed WEDGEWOOD. Made by W. Smith and Co of Stockton-on-Tees some time before 1848.

278

279

280

278 Large jug transfer printed in blue with an engraving showing John Blenkinsop's locomotive and train of coal wagons on the viaduct at Leeds. Christ Church, Leeds, on the other side. Possibly made in Leeds or at the Don Pottery. *c.* 1812. Height 8½″. *Collection: Nicholas Meinertzhagen*

279 Frog mug transfer printed in black with a design showing the *Rocket* and *Northumbrian* and the Liverpool Exchange Buildings. Inside the *Novelty* and carriages for passengers as well as a portrait of Queen Adelaide. The transfers are copied from prints by W. Crane *Eight Views illustrating the Liverpool and Manchester Railway* (Chester) 1830. Unmarked but possibly made at the Herculaneum Factory, Liverpool. *c.* 1830. Height 4⅝″. *Collection: Nicholas Meinertzhagen*

280 Left: Mug transfer printed in dark red showing the *William the Fourth* locomotive. (Built by Braithwaite and Ericsson in 1830). On the Liverpool and Manchester Railway. Unmarked but probably Leeds. 1830. Height 3¾″. *Collection: Nicholas Meinertzhagen*

Right: Jug transfer printed in lilac. Entrance to the Liverpool and Manchester Railway. The shape of this jug, though not uncommon, is rarely found with railway transfer decoration. Probably made in Staffordshire. *c.* 1830. Unmarked. Base Dia. 3⅛″.

148

14 Railway commemorative transfer-printed pottery

The nineteenth century was the great age of steam–the Railway Age–the age of cheap and popular travel. The potteries cashed in on this by making railway souvenirs in great quantities for the travelling public to buy. The opening of a new line, the introduction of a new locomotive, the building of a new bridge were all seized upon by the designers of transfers. The opening of the Liverpool and Manchester Railway was the most commemorated event of all.

The railway pottery was nearly all of a fairly crude quality, but as always there were exceptions. However, today, even the crudest of these pieces are of interest to the collector, not only of nineteenth century pottery, but of railway relics as well.

These railway pieces were made to be used: mugs, jugs, bowls and plates are most often found; they are seldom in good condition being chipped, cracked and discoloured as though they had been subjected to hard wear. As they must have been made very cheaply and in large quantities, obviously they were little valued at the time.

The manufacture of this railway commemoration pottery began before Queen Victoria came to the throne. The first railway was bringing coal to Leeds from the Middleton Colliery by about 1812 (incidentally passing the site of the Leeds Pottery), and Blenkinsop's engine with its train of coal trucks is the first locomotive to be illustrated on pottery. The *William the Fourth, Novelty, Rocket, Fury, Express* and many more followed.

Rather more sophisticated pieces were made by such firms as those of Enoch Wood and Minton. The Wood factory produced some beautiful dark blue transfer-decorated plates with American railway scenes (the Baltimore and Ohio railroad being one of them), bordered by the same shell design as on page 146, which they exported in large shipments to the New World.

Very many small factories in Staffordshire produced railway commemorative pieces, though they by no means always marked their ware. It was also made in potteries in Sunderland and Stockton-on-Tees and Newcastle-upon-Tyne. The greatest quantity of railway ware was produced between 1830 (the opening of the Liverpool and Manchester Railway) and 1850, though other pieces were made right through the nineteenth century and as late as 1925.

A few of the main producers of railway pottery
Ellis, Unwin and Mountford, Unwin Mountford and Taylor *c.* 1864–65. Edge Malkin & Co 1871. Ford Challinor & Co 1855. Jackson & Gosling, Wood Challinor, and W. Smith and Co of Stockton-on-Tees 1825–55. Enoch Wood and Sons 1830's.

281

282

281 Sauceboat of almost white earthenware, decorated with a black transfer showing the jollifications at the opening of the Liverpool and Manchester Railway. Pink lustre bands top and bottom. *c.* 1830. Probably made in Liverpool, but unmarked. Height 3½″.

282 Left: Quart mug transfer printed in black with a design showing the entrance to the Liverpool and Manchester Railway. This view of the Moorish Arch is taken from Henry Booth's *An Account of the Liverpool and Manchester Railway* 1st Edition 1830.
The *Novelty* was built by Braithwaite and Ericsson and took part in the famous Rainhill Trials. Unmarked. 1830. Base Dia. 5⅛″.
Right: Blue transfer printed mug showing the *London* locomotive L. & M.R. The three coaches the other side called *Victoria, Coronation* and *London Royal Mail Liverpool*. 1837, the year of Queen Victoria's Coronation and the partial opening of the main lines from London to Liverpool and Manchester. Unmarked. Height 4⅞″. *Collection: Nicholas Meinertzhagen*

150

283 284

285

283 Plate transfer printed in red and green with a view of the Moorish Arch of the Liverpool and Manchester Railway. Marked E.W. & S. in a shield with a lion crest. (Enoch Wood and Sons, Burslem). *c.* 1830. Dia. 9″. *Collection: Nicholas Meinertzhagen*

284 Railway jug made by Minton. Designed by Henry Townsend. On the front are scrolls with 'present' and 'past' with two drivers underneath, a steam locomotive and a coach. Marked Minton 295 & 6. White figures in relief on a brown background. This is actually made in stoneware–a white version of the jug, showing the other side appears on page 74. 1848. Height 8½″. *Collection: Sir Arthur Elton*

285 Bowl transfer printed in sepia. The *Fury* locomotive on the L. & M.R. The *Fury* was built by Fenton Murray in August 1831. Bowls of this type are very rare, though mugs are common enough. Marked on base 'Railway' on a scroll and J. & R.G. (John and Robert Godwin, Cobridge, Staffs 1834–66). Base dia. 3⅜″. *Collection: Nicholas Meinertzhagen*

15 Stone China

Cream-coloured earthenware had been superseded by earthenware with a much whiter body. The 'pearl white' ware with its rather dull greyish tinge that Wedgwood in 1779 had considered a change rather than an improvement, though made by the Leeds pottery and by other potteries in Staffordshire, never really caught the public fancy. Before going on to look at the transfer-decorated and lustre ware of the nineteenth century, we must just go back to the early 1800's and take a brief look at something that did capture the public imagination, and this was 'stone china'. It was not 'china' (or rather porcelain) at all, as it was not translucent, it was merely a rather harder and more durable earthenware.

The Turners of Lane End were the first potters to experiment with this new body; they added a new ground stone to the clay, and patented their invention in 1800. This 'patent' stone was called 'Tabberner's Mine Rock' or 'Little Mine Rock' and they first obtained it from some land belonging to the Marquis of Stafford. If he had not stopped them using the stone, the Turners might never have gone bankrupt (as they did in 1806).

Spode and Adams bought up some of the Turners' moulds. Josiah Spode II had also been making 'stone china' since 1805, this was decorated with designs of a mainly oriental character, for the Neo-classicism of the mid-eighteenth century had given way to a fashion for Chinoiserie, the culminating triumph of which can be seen in the Royal Pavilion at Brighton.

But the most famous of all the stone china was made by the Masons of Lane Delph. In 1813, Charles James Mason (whose father had first imported and then made porcelain), patented a strong, hard earthenware very like that produced by Spode and he called it 'Mason's Patent Ironstone China'. This was a brilliantly successful name as it sounded not only strong and reliable, but superior as well, and it at once appealed to the public. Mason's designs were robust in the extreme, cribbed or adapted from oriental originals, with strong bright colours, often with the addition of gilding. In addition to table ware he made large vases and other decorative pieces including four-poster beds and fireplace surrounds, the latter sometimes in a heavy rococo style. For some time the business prospered and great fortunes were made for the Mason family. Eventually labour troubles broke out and in 1848 the whole concern was sold up. He had been declared bankrupt. However, by 1851, he was at work again, this time in a small factory at Longton. He exhibited some specimens of his Patent Ironstone China at the Crystal Palace, but in spite of this, he never really recovered from his financial failure. He gave up work in 1854 and died two years later. The history of the Masons makes fascinating reading.* The Mason moulds and patterns were acquired by Francis Morley (a distant descendant of the Morley who had made stoneware in Nottingham and whose trade card is shown on page 55), and some of them have been

*The Masons of Lane Delph: Reginald G. Haggar. Privately published, 1952

286

287

286 Plate printed with the Willis pattern on glaze in light sepia brightly enamelled by hand with bead below shoulder in gold. Marked 2147 in red and SPODE STONE CHINA. *c.* 1807. Dia. 9½″. *Collection: R.R. J. Copeland* CBE, DL, JP

287 Plate printed with the Peacock pattern on glaze in light sepia brilliantly enamelled by hand, bead at edge and shoulder in gold. Marked 2083 in red and SPODE STONE CHINA. *c.* 1806. Dia. 9½″. *Collection: R.R.J. Copeland* CBE, DL, JP

288 Ironstone mug. The royal blue ground is ornamented with gilt stars. Reserve panels in polychrome enamels. The rim painted with a diaper pattern border in red and gilt with reserve panels in puce. Marked 'Turner's Patent' in red. *c.* 1805. Height 6″. *City Museum, Stoke-on-Trent*

288

in use ever since. Francis Morley had married a Ridgway (another famous potting family) and when his father-in-law retired he took on his business. It was Morley, who, in 1840 had introduced the use of lithographic printing into the ceramic industry. He took into partnership a young man called Taylor Ashworth, whose descendants own the firm today. They still produce many of the traditional Mason designs and until recently traded under the name of Geo. L. Ashworth & Brothers. They now use the name Mason's Ironstone China Ltd.

289

290

291

289 Mason family group. Oil painting by an unknown artist. Left to right Miles Mason, Ruth Mason (née Farrar) his wife. Ann Ruth Mason, daughter, Charles James Mason, in front. George Miles Mason, William Mason, extreme right. *Collection: the late J. V. Goddard Esq*

290 Miniature ironstone fireplace surround, painted on glaze in red and green. Made by Miles Mason. *c.* 1845. Height 12″. *City Museum, Stoke-on-Trent*

291 Vase, ironstone china, elaborately painted and gilded. Marked by G. M. & C. J. Mason. Marked Mason's Patent Ironstone China impressed. *c.* 1820. Height 14½″. *Mason's Ironstone China Ltd*

292

293

292 Two pieces from a very large dinner service made in ironstone china. Hand painted in very striking colours, rich dark blue, greens, pink and oranges, with the addition of gilding. One of the typical Japan patterns of the period 1813–25. Plate marked MASONS PATENT IRONSTONE CHINA impressed. Dia. $9\frac{1}{2}''$. Jug marked IRONSTONE WARRANTED and a crown, blue underglaze transfer probably made later to match. Height $6\frac{1}{2}''$.

293 Two small jugs decorated in a rich royal blue and gold. The one on the right marked MASONS PATENT IRONSTONE CHINA impressed. *c.* 1813–25. Height $4\frac{1}{2}''$. The other unmarked. Height $3\frac{3}{4}''$.

294

295

296

294 Shell decorated with splashed pink lustre of the type known as 'Moonlight' or 'Holy door marble'. Made by Wedgwood. *c.* 1805. Length 10″. *Victoria and Albert Museum*

295 Creamware jug with a slightly blue tinged glaze, decorated with bands of silver lustre and black transfer printed medallions hand painted with enamel colours, pink, yellow, blue and green. Staffordshire. *c.* 1810. Height 5½″.

296 Fine white earthenware figure of a Hussar, coated with silver lustre. Probably made by Richard Wilson at Hanley. *c.* 1810. Height 10¼″. *British Museum*

16 Lustre decorated earthenware

Although lustre decoration had long been used on Spanish pottery, and pottery of this type was imported in quite large quantities into England during the eighteenth century, it was not until nearly the end of that century that the technique was used over here, and it was not until the early nineteenth century that lustre decorated pottery was made on a commercial scale. It is unfortunate both for the collector and the student, that very little lustre decorated pottery is marked.

There were three basic types of lustred pottery, silver (derived from platinum), bronze, copper or gold lustre (all derived from gold) and pink or purple lustre made from a gold powdered compound called Purple of Cassius.

The lustre decoration was used in different ways, over the whole surface of an object, in imitation of metal; it was used with a 'resist' where the pattern was painted on to the surface with sugar dissolved in the painting medium. Wherever the painting occurred the lustre was prevented from adhering and when the painting was washed off after the lustre coating had been applied, the pattern showed white (or whatever the colour of the ground) against the metallic surface. Sometimes the lustre was used in bands in conjunction with other forms of decoration painted, transferred or embossed.

Platinum was not discovered until 1750 and it was not used in the decoration of ceramics until nearly fifty years later, though John Hancock (who was apprenticed to Duesbury of Derby, who also worked with the Swansea factory and with the Turners at Lane End before settling down at Spode's factory) claimed in a letter that he wrote in 1846, to have discovered the lustre technique, which he put into practice while he was working at Spode's. The Spode factory in actual fact, seems to have produced very little lustre ware. There are a few jugs with gold lustre banded necks marked Spode, but no marked silver lustre pieces.

Josiah Wedgwood had experimented with lustre, but it was not until after his death that the firm started to make the pink 'moonlight' lustre (using Purple of Cassius) which Josiah Wedgwood II referred to as 'Holy door marble'. This was about 1805–15. About the same time the firm was making a small amount of copper lustre.

Also in Staffordshire, the firm of Wood and Caldwell produced some solid gold lustre figures and Batkin and Bailey made some silver lustred ware including some curious wigstands. Riddle and Bryan of Longton also made copper lustre. Ridgways made teapots and candlesticks in shapes copied from those of the silversmith in about 1820, and there is, in the Victoria and Albert Museum, a particularly beautiful silver lustre coffee pot of this type, marked with a mysterious anchor mark. This was known as 'poor man's silver'. It was also made in Swansea (from about 1820–40) and in Sunderland at about the same time. After this, the newly introduced technique of electro-plating made the silver lustre less popular and production ceased.

297

298

297 A collection of copper lustred ware showing different treatments of decoration. Made in Sunderland in the early nineteenth century. Height of largest jug 6¼″. *Sunderland Museum*

298 Copper lustre mugs with a white band decorated with purple transfers. Exactly the same transfer as on a Swansea goblet in same copper lustre. c. 1820. Height 3⅛″.

Some fine silver 'resist' pieces were made in Staffordshire and at Leeds, with elaborate patterns that incorporated birds and vines. The lustre decoration was not referred to in any of the Leeds pattern books until 1819 (a year before the pottery became bankrupt) though it may well have been made there earlier.

Ford and Pattersons pottery at Newcastle-upon-Tyne made some pink lustre

299 Group of silver lustred ware, made in imitation of
silver ware (Poor man's silver). Made in Sunderland.
c. 1820–30. Teapot height 6½". *Sunderland Museum*

300 Silver lustre jug decorated with a resist pattern. Made
in Staffordshire. *c.* 1810–20. *Victoria and Albert
Museum*

painted ware decorated with free-hand stylized landscapes. Sewell of Newcastle
also made pink lustre decorated pottery.

The firms of Dixon Austin, Dixon Phillips and Co, Dawson & Co, Low Ford
Pottery and Scott and Sons all made lustred wares in Sunderland in the 1820–40
period.

301

302

301 Two jugs decorated in pink lustre. The one on the left painted in the style typical of the Patterson Pottery (formerly Ford and Patterson 1820–30) Sherriff Hill, Newcastle. Pottery in existence 1830–1904. This is probably about 1850. The other jug very similar in shape, decorated with black hand painted transfers, time of the Crimean War. c. 1854. Smallest jug 4¼″ high.

302 A collection of Sunderland jugs. The top row are all from the Garrison pottery, the second from the right is marked Dixon & Co Sunderland 1813. The jug on the bottom row on the left is from Dawson's pottery, the centre probably Garrison Pottery and the 'Crimea' jug on the right hand bottom is from Scotts Pottery. Early to mid-nineteenth century. The height of largest jug 10¾″. *Sunderland Museum*

opposite MOSAIC WARE

303 Jug of 'Mosaic' ware. Probably Scotts Pottery, Sunderland. Unmarked. Yellow transfer on glossy brown glaze. c. 1830. Height 5¾″.

304 Coffee pot, dish and two tiles made in the distinctive brown ware with a yellow transfer that was used at the Southwick Pottery by the Scott Brothers, called 'Mosaic' ware. The dish is marked SCOTT BROTHERS impressed. c. 1830–64 Width of dish 11″. *Sunderland Museum*

17 Mosaic ware

303

304

Among more ordinary wares, a very distinctive type of transfer-decorated pottery was made at the Southwick Pottery, Sunderland. This was earthenware covered with a shiny brown glaze and transfer-printed in yellow, giving a curious but rather pleasing photographic negative effect. The Southwick Pottery from 1800 to 1890 was in the hands of a family called Scott. They variously marked their wares A. Scott and Co, Scott Southwick, Scott and Sons, Scott Brothers and a good many more variations. Some of the marks were impressed, some printed. These marks have been frequently confused with the Scott Brothers who had a pottery at Portobello near Edinburgh *c.* 1786–96. However it seems more than likely that the brown and yellow pottery referred to above was made a good deal later than 1796.

When the Southwick Pottery shut down, the family presented the Sunderland Museum with a range of these pieces which they called 'Mosaic Ware'. Certain proof that they were not made at the Scottish factory.

305

306

307

308

309

162

18 F & R Pratt and Co of Fenton

MULTI-COLOURED TRANSFER-DECORATED POT LIDS

Before the days of plastic or cardboard containers and cartons, potted meats and relishes, sauces and pomades were packed into attractive pots made of white earthenware with decorative lids.

Felix Edwards Pratt (1813–94), the son of the Felix Pratt of Lane Delph, whose factory had produced some of the distinctive underglaze coloured pottery mentioned in an earlier section of this book, was one of the first potters to make use of multi-colour transfer printing. By 1847, the factory was decorating earthenware pot lids as well as jars for mustards and sauces, etc. Most of the designs were done by Jesse Austin, an artist who worked with Pratt for many years.

Austin was also an engraver, and he engraved the copper plates from which the transfer prints were taken. He usually used three or four colours and a dark brown or black. H.G.Clarke⋆ gives a graphic account of how the designs were transferred to the lids. Apparently the colours were transferred separately one after another, with the key drawing last. How the girls who put the transfers down got them to register is something of a mystery, in spite of the registration marks which were afterwards removed. They were applied at the biscuit stage, then the lid was dipped in glaze and refired. If gold was used, a third firing was necessary. Altogether a long and complicated process for mere packaging. That the lids were appreciated for their aesthetic qualities is obvious by the number that survive today, for they have become collectors' pieces and their value, like that of so much old English pottery has increased tenfold in the last few years.

The earliest lids were for pots of bears' grease, a pomade for the hair; and the enterprising shrimpers of Pegwell Bay ordered them by the hundred for packing their shrimps and fish pastes. These, naturally, were illustrated with fishing scenes and views of the place. The Great Exhibition of 1851 was commemorated on many lids and there were royal portraits, portraits of celebrities, country scenes, animals, birds, shells, flowers and engravings of famous pictures.

Pratt's rivals were T.J. & J.Mayer and John Ridgway and Co. On Jesse Austin's death in 1879, the process virtually came to an end.⋆

⋆The Pictorial Pot Lid Book: H.G.Clarke, Courier Press, London, 1960

305 The Village Wedding an engraving by Jesse Austin after a picture by D. Teniers the younger (1610–1694). Registered by F.R.Pratt and Co January 15 1857. Very rare. Dia. $4\frac{3}{16}''$.

306 Hauling in the Trawl engraving from an original watercolour drawing by Jesse Austin. One of the Pegwell Bay Shrimpers' pot lids. Rare. Undated. Dia. $4\frac{3}{16}''$.

307 A fix from Jesse Austin's original drawing adapted from J.Burnet's painting Playing Draughts. Exceptionally rare. Undated. Dia. $4\frac{3}{16}''$.

308 Guiseppi Garibaldi with the dome of St Peters' Rome behind him. c. 1865. Dia. $4\frac{3}{16}''$. Collection: Hugh Green

309 A relish or mustard pot of pale blue earthenware with a two colour transfer decoration (black and yellow) depicting a hunting scene. Registered at the Patent Office Design Registry on 18 August 1871. Height $3\frac{7}{8}''$.

310
311 312

19 Mocha ware

An intriguing but cheap and essentially utilitarian kind of ware was made during the nineteenth century, called 'Mocha' ware. This was called after Mocha stone or moss agate (originally from Mocha in Arabia) which the type of decoration was supposed to resemble. Mocha ware is said to have originated at the factory of William Adams at Cobridge in the eighteenth century, who used this decoration on cream-coloured earthenware.

The nineteenth century Mocha ware was a cheap, thick, white earthenware and was mainly made for use in public houses. The earliest dated piece is in Christchurch Mansion, Ipswich and is inscribed 1799. Jugs and tankards are the most commonly found items, but other things such as coffee-pots, porringers and butter dishes were also made.

The basis of the design was a broad band of coloured slip, usually blue, grey, or coffee-coloured, and on this band were the 'trees' or moss agate decorations. The potter used a secret mixture, which he called 'tea' which was said to consist of tobacco juice, turpentine, manganese and urine. While his band of colour was still damp, he dropped a small quantity of this curious mixture on to the slip, this then spread out into tree-like fronds (like the marking in moss agate) which contrasted well with the coloured band on the white earthenware. Sometimes black rings were added above and below the coloured area.

Sometimes the decorator has used his 'tea' more lavishly, resulting in a beautiful woodland landscape (opposite).

Ware of this type was illustrated in one of the pattern books belonging to the Leeds Pottery and it was made in Burslem by Edge and Malkin from 1871 to 90 and by T. G. Green and Co of Church Gresley in Derbyshire (founded in 1864 and still working). It is rare, however, to find marked pieces.

310 Tankard with the excise mark and word IMPERIAL sprigged on. (It actually holds $\frac{3}{4}$ pint). The central coloured band of slip is coffee coloured, those at top and bottom are blue, with black rings. Typical Mocha decoration applied as four 'trees'. Unmarked, but probably made by T. G. Green Church, Gresley. 19th century. Height 5″. Jug similar. *Collection: Pamela Pearce*

311 Coffee pot with mocha stone decorations on a coffee coloured ground. Mid 19th century. Height 11$\frac{3}{4}$″. *City Museum, Stoke-on-Trent*

312 Tankard with blue-green slip background and Mocha decoration applied liberally to form a wooded landscape. Mid 19th century. Height 5″. *Collection: Pamela Pearce*

313

20 Measham ware

The pottery associated with the picturesque canal 'narrow' boats dates only from the last quarter of the nineteenth century. Much of this ware (sometimes called Measham ware) was made at Church Gresley in Derbyshire. Pieces occur marked 'Mason Cash Co Church Gresley', though such marked pieces are extremely uncommon. The Victoria Pottery at Woodville quite near Church Gresley also made this type of ware.*

There used to be a shop on the Ashby-de-la-Zouche canal at Measham, on what the bargemen call the Moira Cut; this was also near Church Gresley and the barge folk could order from this shop special pieces inscribed with the names of friends or relations. These were put on by impressing printers' type into the damp clay. Often homely mottos are to be found such as 'Love at Home' or 'Remember Me'. Some teapots are impressed with 'Diamond Jubilee 1887'.

The ware is dark brown and covered with a shiny 'Rockingham' glaze, except where the impressed flowers and birds in white clay are sprigged on, and these are painted with blue, green and pink.

The most spectacular objects made in this type of ware were immense teapots, some as high as 16″, and holding half a gallon of tea. These pots were surmounted by another little teapot, in the form of a knob to the lid.

Kettles and chamberpots, jugs and tobacco jars are also found. Production of this naive but interesting ware ceased about 1910.

*According to the late Mr Pascoe Tunnicliffe, whose father once owned the Woodville Pottery. There is also a letter in the Stoke on Trent Museum, from a lady whose mother used to work on these kind of teapots at Newcastle under Lyme. She said that the painting of the flowers and birds was done by the men in the pottery and not the women. The pottery has not been identified.

313 Measham ware teapot with relief decorations sprigged on. The teapot is covered with a shiny brown Rockingham glaze and the flowers and birds are painted in blue, pink and green. 'A PRESENT FROM A FRIEND' is impressed and filled in with blue. Unmarked, but probably made in Church Gresley. c. 1890. Height 16″.

314
315

316

314 Three jugs, two of which are inscribed 'LOVE AT HOME' impressed blue type. Brown shiny glaze and flowers picked out in blue, green and pink. All unmarked, but probably Church Gresley. *c.* 1890. Height of tallest jug 8″.

315 Tobacco jar, teapot and small jug in the form of an owl. All similar to the jugs above. The owl jug is interesting in that the inscription 'HAFODLWYFOG' is the name of a farm near Nant Gwynant in Snowdonia, well-known to climbers. The ware was obviously not entirely confined to the people on the canal barges. Height of Teapot $7\frac{3}{4}$″; Tobacco jar 7″; Jug $4\frac{5}{8}$″.

316 Chamber pot of Measham ware, the interior washed with white slip and decorated with an array of frogs and lizards. Round the rim is the couplet 'Pick me up and use me well
                                  And what I see I never will tell'
Obviously from the same pottery as the teapots, the circular flower is identical. Height $5\frac{1}{2}$″.
Collection : Hugh Green

317

318

317 A pair of equestrian figures, Queen Victoria and Prince Albert. *c.* 1840. Height 6½".

318 Four unnamed figures, the one on the left obviously intended for Admiral Lord Nelson; a Scottish shepherd and shepherdess and a man with bunches of grapes, probably intended to be an Italian. All of the 1840–50 period, all approx 10½" high. *Collection: Hugh Green*

170

21 Victorian cottage pots and portrait figures

WHITE EARTHENWARE MANTLEPIECE ORNAMENTS DECORATED
WITH ENAMEL COLOURS

At about the time of Queen Victoria's marriage, in 1840, some new and quite distinctive kinds of pottery figures were manufactured. These were unlike any kind of ornament that had been made before, both in form and style and in the actual body of the ware itself.

These mantlepiece ornaments were made in great numbers, largely for an unsophisticated market, for the parlours of cottages and the nurseries, school rooms and kitchens of the well-to-do.* They were made in Staffordshire and also at some of the Scottish potteries, but they are very rarely marked with a maker's name.

They were very simply but ingeniously moulded, most of them having an almost flat back with little modelling or colouring. They were usually mounted on a simple oval base that was much more part of the figure than were the rocky or square bases of the preceding period. In fact, these Victorian figures owed nothing to the porcelain figures of the eighteenth century or to the Walton type of earthenware figures of the beginning of the nineteenth.

The most distinctive colour used on these figures was a rich dark glossy blue; pink, green, orange, black and other colours including gold were sometimes used. Some of the later figures (after about 1860) were decorated only with black, gold and a pale flesh pink. As well as the human figures, models of animals were much in demand and every Victorian kitchen must have had its pair of spaniels flanking the kitchen clock. Greyhounds, poodles, dalmatians and more rarely cats were made, as well as more exotic creatures like zebras. Particularly spirited large spaniels were made in Sunderland, often with copper lustre patches on their bodies, or lustred chains round their necks. Churches, cottages and castles were also made in a profusion of designs. Even railway engines were made in this type of pottery.

The most interesting figures, though, were the naive portrait figures many of which are actually named, and through which one can trace much of the social and military history of the Victorian era. The names on these figures were usually in relief on the front of the base, or written on in a cursive hand in gold letters, or very occasionally impressed from printers' type.

Amongst some of the earliest of this type of white earthenware figure were portraits of Queen Victoria and Prince Albert, though other members of the Royal family are also found, standing, sitting and even mounted on horseback.

*In August 1868, in *Punch*, Charles Keene drew a pair of equestrian Staffordshire figures on a mantlepiece with 'an aesthetic gentleman' begging his ferocious-looking landlady to 'remove those fictile abominations'.

Likenesses of various politicians including Sir Robert Peel and the Duke of Wellington also appeared. The Crimean War (1854) created a demand for portrait figures of many of the personalities involved in that disastrous and incompetent campaign. The Queen with the Sultan of Turkey and Napoleon III, the King of Sardinia with Prince Albert, British and French admirals, Turkish and British generals and Miss Nightingale standing stiffly beside a wounded soldier. The Indian Mutiny inspired figures of Sir Colin Campbell, General Sir Henry Havelock and Highland Jessie; the American Civil War–figures of John Brown and Abraham Lincoln. Garibaldi visited England in 1864 and this visit inspired about a dozen different portrait models of the great man, with and without a horse. The Franco-Prussian War of 1870 inspired portraits of various German personalities, but by then the characteristic Staffordshire blue had almost ceased to be used and the figures were less colourful. The wars in Egypt and South Africa were commemorated by portrait figures of General Gordon, Lord Kitchener and General Buller.

Apart from royal, naval and military characters, evangelists such as Moody and Sankey were represented showing another facet of Victorian life; while the shadier side of society was shown by portraits of criminals and their victims. Well known poets, prize fighters, singers, actors, lion-tamers and jockeys all found their way on to the Victorian mantlepiece. Many of the portrait figures were made in different sizes from about eight inches to fourteen or fifteen inches high.

Fictitious characters such as Uncle Tom and Little Eva and Romeo and Juliet were also represented and religious and historical subjects were also popular. Apostles and saints jostled with a crowd of anonymous country people, goatherds, gipsies, fishermen, shepherds, lovers in arbours.

After the death of Queen Victoria, the last of these types of portrait figures were made in the likenesses of Edward VII and Queen Alexandra and Princess May (Queen Mary).

Practically none of these Victorian figures is marked, but a figure of Robert Burns has been found with S. Smith Longton on it, Lord Roberts with Hanley/Lancasters Limited/England, and Edward VII and Queen Alexandra with I. H. Sandland.

Mr Balston has isolated two factories, which he calls the 'Alpha' and the 'Tallis' factories, where two distinct and definite types of figure were made.* The Alpha factory mostly used printer's type for impressing the name on to the stand, and the Tallis factory were responsible for the Shakespearean characters modelled from the engravings in the Tallis Shakespeare Gallery (1852–3) and some other figures in the same style. These are made of a hard and heavy body and are modelled and painted on the back as well as the front, some having indented titles in capital letters or transfer titles. None have raised lettering or gilt script.

Sampson Smith, who must have been the most prolific of the makers of flat-backed figures, was working from *c.* 1847–78, and his factory went on making

---

Staffordshire Portrait Figures of the Victorian Age: T. Balston, Faber 1958 and John Hall's supplement to this book.

319 Benjamin Franklin (1706–90) American Statesman, sent to England on a political mission in 1757. He failed to reconcile the colonies with Great Britain and later negotiated an alliance with France. This figure is taken from the same model as George Washington, but Washington is usually larger. Enoch Wood is said to have made a standing figure of Franklin. These may well be copied from that. (The Wood firm certainly had a large export trade to America). 1846–53 period. Height 14″. *Victoria and Albert Museum*

320   321   322

323   324

them after his death. In 1948, the descendants of the firm discovered a number of original moulds in a disused part of the factory; dogs and cottages as well as figures. The trade was revived though the colouring was not so pleasing as that on their predecessors.

Lancaster and Sandlands are making some of the old models today. They have taken great pains to try to match the old rich Staffordshire blue. They are also making cottages and animals. The factory are turning out honest reproductions; one only hopes that the dealers into whose hands they fall are as honest in their transactions, for the reproductions are quite good enough to fool the embryo collector.

320   The Death of Nelson, with the title in gilt script. The uniform jackets are the characteristic dark shiny blue. *c.* 1840. Height 8½″. *Collection: Natalie Bevan*

321   Queen Victoria and Prince Albert. Probably made soon after their marriage. *c.* 1840. Height 8½″.

322   George Washington (1732–99) from the same model as Benjamin Franklin (see page 173). 1846–53 period. Height 15½″. *Collection: John Hall*

323   Death of the Lion Queen (Ellen Bright 1832–50). Ellen was the neice of George Wombwell the circus proprietor. She became the 'Lion Queen' at the age of 16 and was mauled to death at Chatham by a tiger a year later. 1850. Height 15″. *Collection: Mrs F. Cashmore*

324   Queen Victoria with Abdul Medjid, Sultan of Turkey and the Emperor Napoleon III. This commemorates the alliance made between the three countries at the time of the Crimean War. 1854. Height 10¾″. *Collection: Natalie Bevan*

325   Omah Pasha (1806–71) was the Commander in Chief of the Turkish forces throughout the Crimean War. 1854. Height 10¾″. *Collection: Mrs F. Cashmore*

326   Prince Albert with Napoleon III standing under each other's national flags. 1854. Height 13¼″. *Collection: John Hall*

327   Admiral Sir Charles Napier (1786–1860) commanded the Baltic Fleet in 1854–55. 1854. Height 9½″. *Willett Collection, Brighton*

328
329

330

328 Sir John and Lady Franklin. Sir John died while trying to discover the North West Passage in 1847. The impressed names and general style shows that these figures were made at what T. Balston called the 'Alpha' factory. *c.* 1847. Height 11¼″. *Willett Collection, Brighton*

329 The Empress Eugenie and the Prince Imperial. The Empress (1826–1920) was wife of Napolean III. Colourless except for pink, black and gilt. 1856. Height 7¾″. *Willett Collection, Brighton*

330 A man with a deer. *c.* 1840–50. Height 8″. Jenny Lind as Maria in *The Daughter of the Regiment*. *c.* 1847. Height 8″. Queen Victoria on a horse, wearing a rich dark blue dress with pink, black and yellow. *c.* 1840. Height 7″. One of a pair with Albert.

176

331

332

331 Dick Turpin and Tom King, the notorious eighteenth-century highwaymen, popularized by Harrison Ainsworth in his novel *Rookwood* published 1834. *c.* 1850. Height 12″. *Willett Collection, Brighton*

332 James Rush, the murderer, Potash Farm, his house and Emily Sandford his mistress whose evidence helped convict him. Rush was hanged outside Norwich Castle in 1849. *c.* 1850. Height of figures 10¼″. *Willett Collection, Brighton*

333
334

178

335

333 Pair of spaniels with black patches and gold chains round their necks. These were made in Staffordshire by Sampson Smith and other potters, and also in Sunderland. Greyhound probably made in Staffordshire. *c.* 1850–60. Spaniels 10¼" high.

334 A pair of dancers and an archer, dressed in green, probably intended for Robin Hood. *c.* 1850–60. Height 10".

335 Highland Jessie. An almost legendary figure. The wife of Corporal Brown (no doubt standing beside her) who inspired the garrison at Lucknow to hold out, by screaming out that she could hear pipes playing 'The Campbells are coming'. The garrison was relieved. 1857. Height 14½". *Collection: Mrs F. Cashmore*

336
338

337
339

RIVAL

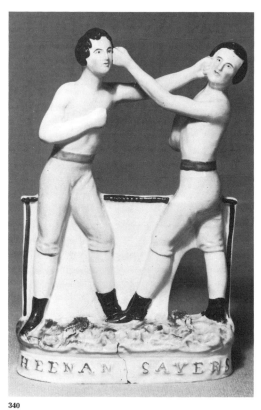

340

341

336 Flower holder. Lovers beneath a tree; the jealous rival eavesdrops. *c.* 1850–60.

337 Arbour group. The jealous rival about to attack the unsuspecting lovers. *c.* 1850–60. Height 10″.

338 Flower holder. A rustic couple beneath a tree. *c.* 1850–60. Height 11½″.

339 Watch-stand. The fortune teller and her two clients. *c.* 1850. Height 11″.

340 Heenan and Sayers, the prize fighters. Probably made after their famous fight at Farnborough in 1860. Height 9½″. *Willett Collection, Brighton*

341 A pair of washerwomen. This piece has a slightly different surface quality to all the other pieces. It might be from one of the Scottish potteries, but it is unmarked. *c.* 1850. Height 10¼″.

342

343

342 The Sailor's Return. A popular subject in Victorian England. *c*. 1850. Height 12½".

343 A large and very well-modelled figure. The sheep are covered with a sprinkling of granules of clay to simulate wool. *c*. 1850. Height 14".

344 The Flight into Egypt, so inscribed with a gilt script on the base. Colourless group except for touches of black, pink and gilt. *c*. 1860–70.

345 Garibaldi (1807–82), The Liberator of Italy. After his visit to England in 1864, he became extremely popular and many portrait figures were made of him, both with and without his horse. *c*. 1864. Height 14". *Collection: John Hall*

344
345

GARIBALDI

346

347

346 Tea-set designed by Sir Henry Cole (Felix Summerly) and made by Mintons in 1846. This was the tea-set that won the Society of Art prize and gave Cole the idea of starting Summerly's Art Manufactures. *Victoria and Albert Museum*

347 Two Minton Majolica pieces. The seahorse and Cupid group was modelled by A. Carrier de Belleuse and decorated in coloured glazes. It bears the Minton date mark for 1859. Height 16″. *Victoria and Albert Museum*

22 Artist potters

One of the first people in Victorian times who attempted to improve the standard of public taste was Sir Henry Cole. He won a prize given by the Society of Arts in 1846, for the design of a tea-set which he entered for a competition under the pseudonym of Felix Summerly. He started up a company called Summerly's Art Manufactures and tried to persuade well-known painters and sculptors to design for industry. This venture does not seem to have been very successful, for it only lasted three years.

About 1867, Doulton's of Lambeth, under the enlightened leadership of Sir Henry Doulton and with the close co-operation of George Tinworth and some students from the Lambeth School of Art, brought about something like a renaissance in decorative stoneware. George Tinworth also designed and made for them many terracotta panels, mainly bas-reliefs of religious subjects, for the decoration of churches. These were executed with the utmost sincerity and were much admired by the general public as well as by the art critic John Ruskin. Among other artists who worked for Doultons were Hannah, Florence and Arthur Barlow and Mark V. Marshall.

Alfred Stevens was one of the artists who worked for Mintons, for whom he designed a series of earthenware vases. An unlikely artist to work for the pottery industry was Hablot K. Browne (the illustrator of so many of the works of Charles Dickens). Browne designed the transfer decorations for a dinner-service made by Brownfields of Cobridge in 1862.

Wallace Martin, after some training at Lambeth School of Art and working as a sculptor's assistant, went to work at the Fulham Pottery (where John Dwight had worked). In 1873, he set up a workshop in King's Road, Fulham with his two younger brothers, who had been working at Doultons. The firing was done at the Fulham Pottery. Finally in 1877 they moved to Southall. Wallace was the head of the firm and was responsible for the modelling. Walter did most of the throwing, glazing and firing and Edwin did most of the decorating. The other brother Charles ran a shop that they had acquired near High Holborn. Wallace was the originator of the grotesque birds with big beaks and sly eyes as well as the jugs in the shape of human heads with leering expressions. Much of the Martins' early work was blue and grey, later a dark brown was used and later still greens and blues and browns. The colouring was always very low in tone. Relief and incised decoration was used, much of it with floral forms. Some of the later pots and vases were inspired by vegetable forms like gourds and marrows with vertical ribbed designs and textured surfaces. They made many miniature versions of their wares which are particularly attractive and quite as well finished as the larger pots, for the Martins were all expert craftsmen. They worked together perfectly as a team. Charles died in 1910 and Walter in 1912. They were sadly missed by the others. After the death of Edwin in 1914, only one more kiln was fired. Wallace lived on until 1923. Most of their work is marked on the bottom in a cursive hand with the date and the name of the firm. Their pots are now much sought after by collectors.

William de Morgan was perhaps the most outstanding of all the artist potters of the late nineteenth century. He studied at the Academy Schools. He met William Morris and possibly under Morris's influence took up pottery rather than painting. He began in quite a small way making tiles, vases and dishes inspired by Persian pottery and decorated with animals, birds, flowers and fishes in greens, pinks and blues. He also made some fine dishes in a ruby red lustre on a cream-coloured earthenware. Although de Morgan produced a certain amount of beautiful work, he never had very much financial success, though his work became well-known in his life time. In 1888 he went into partnership with the architect Halsey Ricardo and they founded the Sands End Pottery at Fulham, where many of the tiles de Morgan designed were painted. His health was not good, and by 1892 he was obliged to spend the winters abroad, which made organizing the work difficult. By 1907 his health had broken down and he was forced to give up. Among the painters who worked for him were Fred and Charles Passenger, Joe Juster and Jim Hersey. Their initials are frequently to be found on the base of de Morgan pots.

Another potter who was fascinated by colour was Bernard Moore. He and his brother Samuel had taken over their father's factory at Longton in Staffordshire in 1870 and ran it until 1905. After this, he set up as a ceramic consultant. He had always been interested in glazes, particularly those used by potters in the Far East and he became famous for his experiments with these. He produced some technically remarkable pieces with *flambé* and *sang de boeuf* glazes. Until the 1914 war he employed artists to make decorative pieces for exhibitions. His work is signed B M or with his whole name in capital letters.

Towards the end of the century, in 1892, the Pilkington Pottery was established at Clifton Junction near Manchester. To begin with they made glazed bricks and tiles, but soon the pottery began to experiment with decorative ware under the leadership of William and Joseph Burton. During the first two decades of the twentieth century many famous artists designed for them, including Gordon Forsyth, Lewis Day, Walter Crane and Richard Joyce. Experiments were made with many different kinds of glazes and shapes. At one time double-thrown pottery was produced, the outer shape pierced to reveal the inner, the whole being glazed with plain mottled or onyx glaze, though this was discontinued soon after the first world war. Ware was decorated with *sgraffito* decoration and they even experiemented with a kind of Palissy ware encrusted with modelled newts and lizards. But the main feature of the pottery was the variety and beauty of the glazes that were used.

As a reaction to the orientally inspired work of so many potters, others turned to the traditional brown slip-decorated earthenware. One of these potters was Reginald Wells, a sculptor by training, who had taken up pottery about 1909 and produced simple if rather clumsy shapes of a traditional English character.

Just before the first world war Roger Fry started the Omega Workshops, where a small amount of quite pleasant, simply designed ware was produced; but the war made things too difficult and they shut down in 1919.

As well as the artist potters, there is a small group of craftsmen whose work should not be completely ignored. These are the real country potters. Small potteries in obscure villages run by one man with the help, perhaps, of a member or two of his family, their survival depending on producing ware for local use. These men were artists in their way, and made their pots because they liked to do so.

The Fremington Pottery near Bideford in Devon was just this sort of family concern. It was established in the early nineteenth century by George Fishley and passed from father to son, producing *sgraffito* decorated harvest jugs and similar things in a traditional slip-decorated manner. Edwin Beer Fishley, who died in 1912 has left many interesting pieces signed with his name.

Another of these country potteries existed in Essex, in a ramshackle collection of buildings at Castle Hedingham, the walls of which were covered with scriptural texts. There was a small showcase at the end of the garden which bore the inscription 'Original, Quaint and Classical'. This pottery was owned by a somewhat eccentric Plymouth Brother, whose father, also a potter, had settled in Castle Hedingham in the 1830's. Edward Bingham was working from about 1864 to 1905. He made from the local clay, which he and his family dug and refined, the most elaborate pieces with moulded applied decoration, sometimes in white clay with coloured glazes: blue, grey, green and brown. He was interested in history and loved to copy coats of arms and motifs from classical sources. Some of his pieces have an almost surrealist quality. There is an extraordinary teapot in the Victoria and Albert Museum that is nightmarish in its absurdity. Bingham was no business man and found it difficult to market his wares; by the beginning of the twentieth century the pottery was in difficulties and his children emigrated to America. In 1905 he joined them. His ware was marked with a small relief of Hedingham Castle, and usually his initials or signature.

The Rye Pottery was established in the fifteenth century and had throughout its history produced wares of an individual and imaginative nature. About the middle of the nineteenth century the pottery was in the hands of the Mitchell family, who began to make some curious ware decorated with hops. William Mitchell developed this technique to a fine standard of craftsmanship and the naturalistic three-dimensional hops and leaves were glazed with a good green glaze, set off by the dark brown streaked glaze on the body of the ware.

348
349

350

351

348 Painted earthenware vases and plates designed for Mintons by
Alfred Stevens. Inscribed 'February 1864' on the two plates and
the tallest vase. They are all copies of the prototypes that were
made from Steven's' designs and shown at the International
Exhibition of 1862. They were never actually mass produced.
Height of tallest vase 17″. Dia. of plates 11″. *Victoria and
Albert Museum*

349 Stoneware tankard decorated by George Tinworth for Doultons
in 1874. The incised monogram G T appears near the base.
Impressed mark Doulton Lambeth 1874. Height 10⅜″. Two
vases and an owl in stoneware made by the Martin brothers at
Southall Middlesex. The owl was modelled by Wallace Martin.
He made many more grotesque birds than this. *c.* 1899.
Victoria and Albert Museum

350 Four pieces of stoneware by the Martin brothers, each from a
different period. The jug on the left was made by Wallace
Martin in 1874 at the Fulham Pottery. Height 8⅛″. The vase
next to it was made at Southall in 1886. The jug with the
human face was made by Wallace Martin in 1900 at Southall.
Height 8¾″. The vase on the right which is a pleasant green is
typical of their 'vegetable' period and was made by Edwin
Martin in 1903. Height 10″. *Victoria and Albert Museum*

351 Brown salt-glazed stoneware vase by Mark V. Marshall. *c.* 1875.
Height 10″. *Doulton and Co Ltd*

189

352

353

354

355

356

352 Decorative panel of tiles designed by William de Morgan in typical Persian colouring. Probably made at the Sands End Pottery between 1888–98. Each tile is 6″ square. *Victoria and Albert Museum*

353 Plate decorated in ruby lustre by William de Morgan, probably at Merton Abbey between 1882–88. Dia. 14⅜″. *Victoria and Albert Museum*

354 Plate decorated in salmon pink lustre by William de Morgan. Ships were a favourite and recurring theme. *c.* 1890. Dia. 12″.

355 Vase with design by William de Morgan, painted in blues and greens. *c.* 1888. Height 9″.

356 Earthenware dish designed by Lewis F. Day who was a founder member of the Arts and Crafts Exhibition Society. 1877. Dia. 10¼″. *Victoria and Albert Museum*

Photo: Bob Alcock

357 Panel of tiles in typical Persian colouring. Designed by William de Morgan Probably made at the Sands End Pottery between 1888–98. Each tile is 6″ square.

358 Vase made by Bernard Moore. *c.* 1904. Made in a fine hard earthenware with a *sang de boeuf* glaze. The rich, glowing intense red specked with golden lights and the absolutely plain undecorated shape makes an interesting contrast with the de Morgan pottery opposite. Height 9¼″.

358
359

359 Group of vases made by Bernard Moore decorated with *rouge flambé* glaze. *c.* 1904. Height of tallest vase 7½″. *Victoria and Albert Museum*

360

361

362

360 Two vases made by Owen Carter. The one on the left is cast and finished in a red copper glaze with a slight lustre effect. The one on the right is thrown and produced by the same method using a reducing atmosphere in the kiln. Both show the influence of the *art nouveau* movement. *c.* 1906. Height 12″. *Carter, Stabler and Adams*

361 Large lustre jar with a reed pen inscription, designed and painted by Gordon M. Forsyth. *c.* 1910. Height 12½″. Forsyth was working with Pilkingtons from 1906–1920. He signed his work with a device of four scythes interlocked. *Collection: Miss M. Pilkington*

362 Tall slim vase with a band of floral decoration inspired by *l'art nouveau*. This was designed and painted by Gordon M. Forsyth in particularly beautiful shades of blue. *c.* 1907. Height 16½″. *Collection: Miss M. Pilkington*

363

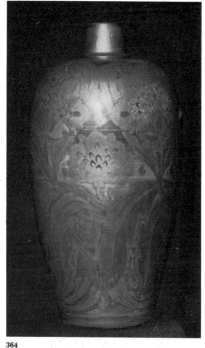

364

365

363 Large lustre jar with a design made up of a frieze of leopards in black, grey and tawny brown. Designed and executed by Richard Joyce. *c.* 1912. Height 9″.
Joyce was at Pilkingtons from about 1906–1931. He was particularly interested in designs based on animal, human and fish forms. He designed some of the best work that the pottery produced.
Collection: Miss M. Pilkington

364 Grey green lustre decorated bottle with an all-over design of conventionalized flowers by Charles Cundall RA. *c.* 1909. Height 9″. *Collection: Miss M. Pilkington*

365 A teacup and saucer and teapot, designed by Roger Fry and made at the Omega Workshops. *c.* 1913. Teapot height 6¼″.

366

367

366 Mantlepiece ornament, probably made by George Fishley at Fremington. *c.* 1860. Height 7″.
Royal Albert Memorial Museum, Exeter

367 Devon harvest pitcher. Decorated in *sgraffito* with birds and flowers inscribed
'Miss Ann Williams Paul may plant and
Appolos water but God gives the increase
Bideford 1866'
White slip on brown clay, glazed with a lead glaze. Height 11″. *Royal Albert Memorial
Museum, Exeter*

368 A group of Mitchell ware made at the Rye pottery by Frederick Mitchell. *c.* 1870. The hops
and leaves are naturalistically coloured and the body of the ware is glazed with a manganese
brown tortoiseshell glaze. Jug 9″ high.

369 A collection of Castle Hedingham ware, made between 1870–1900 by Edward Bingham at
Castle Hedingham. Some of the relief designs are in white clay. The glazes are blue, grey-green,
brown or yellow. The Essex jug at the back shows Boadicea in a chariot on the central medallion
and all round are the arms of Essex families and the symbols of the produce of the county.
Jug 13″ high.

368
369

370

371

372

370 Stoneware vase with *sgraffito* decoration and
temmouko glaze. Made by Bernard Leach.
c. 1957. Height 13½″. *Victoria and Albert Museum*

371 Earthenware jar with slip decoration made by
Michael Cardew *c*. 1950. Height 14⅛″. *Victoria and
Albert Museum*
Michael Cardew learned to throw at the Braunton
Pottery in Devon. He then joined the Leach
pottery, where he worked for three years before
starting up on his own at Winchcombe in
Gloucestershire. This pottery has a kiln large
enough to hold up to three thousand pieces, which
Cardew's energy and drive enabled him to fill
every two or three months. He made mainly useful
slip-decorated earthenware in the English tradition.
He now works in Nigeria.

372 Stoneware vase made by W. Staite Murray.
c. 1938. Height 11½″. *Victoria and Albert Museum*

198

23 The modern artist potter

In the years following the first world war, a number of artist-craftsmen turned their attention to the making of pottery. The inspiration for this came largely from Bernard Leach and William Staite Murray.

Leach had studied the making of stoneware in the Far East, and when he returned to this country in 1920, he set up a pottery near St Ives, with the assistance of a young Japanese potter called Shoji Hamada. For some time Leach made stoneware in the Japanese manner, and then turned his attention to slip-decorated earthenware in the English tradition. Leach trained many pupils at his pottery at St Ives, where he ran a summer school for a small group of students and teachers of pottery. In the early 1930's he started the Shinner's Bridge Pottery at Dartington, before re-visiting the Far East. He then returned to St Ives to the pottery which he ran with a team of potters including his two sons, David and Michael. The Leach Pottery is still producing a steady output of useful ware of a high standard of quality. The Leach influence is still a powerful one.

Staite Murray began to make pottery in 1912; though he attended the Camberwell School of Art for a time, he can be said to have taught himself through his own persistent experiments. In the 1920's he was also influenced by the work of the Japanese potters, and much of his work has an *art nouveau* flavour but is quite unlike that of Leach. Staite Murray managed to persuade some London art dealers to show his work in company with that of the more promising young painters of the time. In this way he contributed much to the idea that studio-potters should be considered as serious artists and not merely as practitioners of a quaint craft. Staite Murray had no interest in the making of useful wares.

In 1925, he was made the head of the ceramic department at the Royal College of Art, where he had a marked influence on many students. In 1940, Staite Murray left England and went to live in Southern Rhodesia. The students who came in contact with Leach and Staite Murray, in addition to producing much interesting work themselves, have passed on their knowledge and interest to another generation of artist potters. Life today is somewhat difficult for these artist craftsmen. Equipment is expensive, the price of fuel is exorbitant and the purchase tax levied on their ware is both iniquitous and crippling. Almost inevitably they have to turn to part-time teaching as a means of livelihood. Whether it is a reaction from the machine age in which we live, the desire to be taught pottery-making is very strong today. The craft is being taught, and taught well, in many schools as well as in art schools. Since the 1930s quite a number of potters from other countries have settled down in England and have made careers for themselves here. As so often in the past we have benefited from this infiltration of foreign talent. We would indeed be the poorer without the work of Hans Coper and Lucie Rie, to name but two of the talented artists now living here.

A trend that has emerged during the last decade is the tendency to turn from the throwing or casting of domestic or useful ware to the making of non-functional pieces that are more akin to sculpture. Pieces that are made simply for the pleasure of the maker and the beholder. The fact that the government has not yet thought fit to put purchase tax on these pieces may have something to do with it, but this seems unlikely, for the potters are not a mercenary lot. They would not be potters if they were.

I have tried to show as wide a range as possible of the work of the last few years, from that of the well-known and established potters to the promising younger generation of today, whose work maybe is less familiar. The productions of small potteries where the work is designed by the principal and carried out by himself and his assistants has also been included, as well as the work of part-time teachers of pottery, and pots made by those who are lucky enough to be able to pursue their craft seriously, but as a hobby. The pictures shown here are a cross-section of the work of only relatively few of our artist potters, but I hope there is enough evidence to show the vitality in the work of these contemporary potters and to suggest to collectors of ceramics that here are pots just as worthy of collection as anything that came from the hands of Toft, Whieldon or Wood.

373 Earthenware bowl with tin-glazed decoration in grey, brown and green made by Steven Sykes. *c.* 1950. Dia. 13″. *Victoria and Albert Museum*
Steven Sykes studied at the Royal College of Art from 1933 to 1936 and later learned the craft of pottery from his wife who had worked under Staite Murray. For a time he taught pottery at the Central School of Art and Design. He has made ceramic tiles which have been used in large scale decorations in the Dorchester Hotel and many other places. His work is owned by the Victoria and Albert Museum, the Otago Museum, New Zealand, and many private collectors.

374 Stoneware bread crock with an unglazed exterior decorated with tooling and seals. The interior is glazed green. Made in 1951 by Paul Barron. Height 14″.
Paul Barron studied at the Brighton School of Art under Norah Braden (a pupil of Leach's) from 1937 to 1939. He now teaches at the Farnham School of Art with Henry Hammond, with whom he also runs the Bentley Pottery.

375 Large stoneware bowl with a celadon glaze inside and brush decorated blue rimmed outside, small stoneware bowl and cylinder vase. Large bowl 16″ dia. Made by Peter O'Malley in 1968.
Peter O'Malley gave up a career as a professional soldier to become a potter. He studied at the Royal College of Art under Professor Baker and then worked at various potteries both in England and on the Continent. He has recently had a show of his pottery in London. He is a tutor in the Ceramic Department at the Royal College of Art.

376 Stoneware bowl with matt glaze and brush stroke decoration in blue. Made by Henry Hammond. Dia. 4″. *British Council*
Henry Fauchon Hammond studied at the Royal College of Art under Staite Murray and was also helped and encouraged by Bernard Leach. He has produced slipware and stoneware, simply decorated, in the Japanese manner. In addition to running a pottery at Bentley near Farnham with Paul Barron and his wife, he is the head of the Ceramic Department at the Farnham School of Art.

377 Stoneware bowl of a warm ochre colour with dark blue-grey brush stroke decoration. Made in 1954 by Henry Hammond. Dia. 5½″.

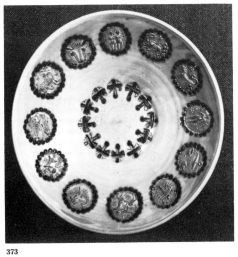

373

374

375
376

377

201

378

378 Goblet set. Made of stoneware and partly glazed with a matt white ash glaze. The clay is rust to oatmeal in colour and the pieces were reduced fired to 1300°. Height of the jug 12″. Made by Robin Welch at Stradbroke in 1969. See page 207.

379 Three stoneware storage jars, the right hand one is greyish in colour, the other two are greenish yellow, with cut decoration. Made by Richard Batterham in 1968. Height 7″ and 5″. Richard Batterham studied pottery under Donald Potter at Bryanston and then went and worked for two years at the Leach Pottery, before setting up his own workshop about ten years ago at Durweston near Blandford Forum in Dorset. He is one of the few craftsmen potters working on his own, who manages to earn a living entirely by the pots he makes, without spending any time teaching. He produces, about 5000 pots a year, each one of which he considers as an individual piece, for he is a perfectionist. His pots are all for domestic use. He uses a number of different clays and different glazes and uses simple incised decoration, resulting in the most satisfying and beautiful pots.

379

380

380 Three mugs, the shapes by Kenneth Clark and the decoration designed by Ann Wynn Reeves. Approx 4″ high.

Kenneth Clark's pottery is in London. He now employs three full time assistants. In addition to teaching one day a week at the Central School of Art and Design, he is retained by a tile manufacturer in Stoke-on-Trent. Much of the work of his pottery is in the form of ceramic murals and ceramic work in interior decoration.

381 Blue-green and grey-green tin-glazed bowl. Dia. 13″. Blue and grey tin-glazed storage jar 8″ high. Both with brush stroke decoration. Made by Alan Caiger-Smith in 1961 at the Aldermaston Pottery. *Council of Industrial Design*

Alan Caiger-Smith studied painting at Camberwell and then went to the Central School of Art and Design to study pottery. He started the Aldermaston Pottery in 1955 and his work has been shown at many exhibitions all over the world. The thriving pottery now consists of about half a dozen people. The pots are made of red earthenware and tin-glazed. Some are electrically fired, but most of them are fired in a slightly reducing atmosphere in a wood fired kiln, which deepens and enriches the traditional range of tin-glaze colours. He is now producing some very beautiful thrice-fired reduced copper and silver lustre decorated pieces.

381

382

383

384

385

382 Shishi, a legendary Japanese animal, inspired by a drawing by Hokusai. White tin-glaze on red earthenware and painted in black. Made by Natalie Bevan in 1967. Height 7".

383 Elephant made of earthenware and tin-glazed with various colours to produce a fine speckled grey effect. Made by Natalie Bevan in 1967. Height 7".
Natalie Bevan worked for some time at the Chelsea Pottery, where she says 'she picked up the rudiments of glazing.' She started working on her own with her own workshop and kiln only a few years ago. She has had various exhibitions, at the Minories Colchester, Essex and in London at the Anthony d'Offay Fine Art Gallery.

384 A group of quail by Anne Gordon made of tin-glazed earthenware and painted in black, yellow, pink and grey and green enamel in the leaves of the supporting trees. Height about 5". Made in 1968.
Anne Gordon learned much about pottery and particularly about tin-glazing from Alan Caiger-Smith at the Aldermaston Pottery. She specializes in naturalistically modelled animals and birds. She had a one-man show in London last year.

385 Stoneware bull and cow made by Eve Borthwick, who studied painting at the Watford School of Art under A.J.B.Sutherland and took up pottery later. Her chief interest is in large terra-cotta groups and figures. These were made in 1956. Height $6\frac{1}{4}$".

386
387

388

386 A collection of stoneware cylinders, the centre section cast aluminium. The sections are treated in various ways with either metallic black glazes and copper textured clay or matt white ash glazes rubbed with copper oxide and fired in a reducing atmosphere to 1300°. Made by Robin Welch in 1969. Height of largest cylinder 48″.
Robin Welch, after studying at the Nuneaton School of Art studied sculpture at the Penzance School of Art, and pottery under Michael Leach. After studying and working as a technical assistant at the Central School of Arts and Crafts in London, he started a pottery workshop of his own in London. He then spent three years establishing a large country workshop near Melbourne in Australia and returned to England in 1965 to start his own pottery workshop at Stradbroke in Suffolk. His work has a strong and essentially sculptural quality. He is certainly one of the most interesting potters of his generation. His work has been exhibited in London, Japan, Scandinavia and Australia, and is in many public and private collections. In addition to his non-functional pieces, he makes useful ware of a very high quality.

387 Coffee set made by Lucie Rie in brown stoneware with *sgraffito* decoration. Glazed white inside. Made in 1969. Coffee pot 7″ high. *Council of Industrial Design*
Lucie Rie studied pottery in Vienna and came to settle in England before the last war. She makes mainly domestic ware of a very delicate and individual character.
Her work has been seen in Exhibitions all over the world, and is in many museums and galleries as well as in private collections.

388 A collection of pots made of white fire clay with added foundry clay and covered in layers of a vitreous slip glaze. Made by Hans Coper in 1968. Height of central foreground pot $6\frac{3}{4}$″.
Hans Coper came to England before the last war. He was trained both as a sculptor and an engineer, which is perhaps reflected in his work which has a strong sculptural quality, at the same time as being intensely precise. For many years he worked with Lucie Rie, but in 1958 he set up his own workshop in London. He recently moved to Somerset where he now works. His pots are to be found in many galleries and private collections throughout the world.

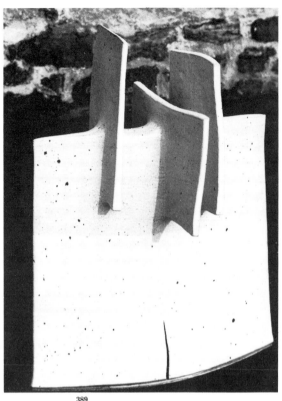

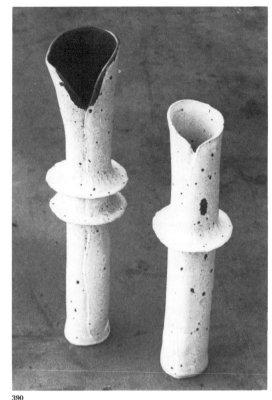

389   390

389 Slabbed and coiled form by James Campbell, who used a white feldspathic glaze containing ball
clay and stealite on the body made of potclays buff and crank mixture. The glaze is creamy in
texture and produces iron specks from the clay underneath. The lighter coloured band across
the centre of the piece is produced by glaze overlap. Made in 1968. 21½″ high.

390 Two slab built tubes with the addition of coiled and pinched flanges. Made of the same clay as
no 389, with a similar white glaze.
The tube on the left has a semi-matt brown/black glaze inside. Made in 1969 by James
Campbell. Heights 15″ and 12″.

391

James Campbell studied at Eton with Gordon
Baldwin and then at the Royal College of Art from
1960–64. In 1968 he set up a workshop in
Herefordshire, where he built a propane fired kiln.
Most of his work consists of hand built (coiled,
slabbed or thumbed) non-functional pieces fired to
stoneware temperature under reduction. His work has
been exhibited in London, Glasgow, Denmark,
Germany, Italy and Australia.

391 A group of three different units in dark brown
stoneware with a yellow brown glaze by David
Robinson, 1969. Height 6″.
David Robinson first studied at Sunderland College
of Art and then at the Royal College of Art. At the
moment, in addition to potting and painting, he
teaches at the West of England College of Art.
James Campbell and David Robinson are producing
some of the most interesting non-functional pottery
being made today.

208

392

392 Unglazed stoneware structure, by David Robinson, 1969. Height 14″.

24 Factory made pottery today

The structure and technology of the English pottery industry is changing rapidly. Until the war, there were literally hundreds of potteries–some small and still relatively primitive–some large and forward thinking. During the last ten years or so, the tendency has been for firms to amalgamate, less to put rivals out of business than to complement each other's activities and to share the ever-growing research and sales organizations. English pottery plays an important part in our economy; it has never been more widely exported than it is today. Now the industry is in the hands of relatively few groups, though there are some small firms carrying on in an independent and traditional way. The old bottle kiln is a thing of the past; the Clean Air Act and the use of gas, electricity and oil have made the use of coal obsolete, and the tunnel kiln has taken over–perhaps to be superseded in its turn by the newly invented hover-kiln. Old, high, congested buildings with dangerously inadequate stairways and fire escapes are being razed to the ground to make room for the long, low buildings that today's production-line output needs.

But the complex modern pottery industry is still essentially a craft industry, dependent on the skill of hand of the worker at each stage of production. In spite of the tremendous advance in mechanization this skill is still very much in evidence, and though each new technical and mechanical advance means the loss of some skilled hand work, and therefore a slight reduction in quality, this is justified by the manufacturers by the fact that they have to increase productivity or go out of business.

An example of this increased productivity, to name but one, has been brought about by the Murray-Curvex process, which consists of printing the engraved patterns from the inked plate to a transfer gelatine mould and straight down on to flat ware. This cuts out many processes and a vast amount of time and labour is saved. The final result is only a little less good than that achieved by the traditional method. But, so far, this process cannot be used on hollow ware.

The revolutionary hover-kiln which can cut down the gloss firing time from about twelve hours to fifteen minutes is something that will bring great savings in fuel and other advantages, as well as enormous problems of reorganization to the manufacturers.

But although traditional methods of production are being revolutionized, as far as design goes, tradition dies very hard indeed. In this century, the designs of the bulk of the pottery that has been made, do not really reflect our way of life and changing tastes; when it comes to our breakfast, dinner and tea services, most of us are escapist. We like to look back at the past, we like what we are used to. Moreover we cannot all afford to scrap our table services every few years; when we do decide to have a change, we want to be assured that we will be able to buy replacements for many years to come. However, there are always some people who want something new, and to whom the latest thing is the best (Josiah

393 394

395

393 *Argosy* pattern on *Olympic* shapes which were designed in 1964. The design by Peter Wall DES RCA, is reproduced in blue on fine white earthenware. Made by Wedgwoods. *Wedgwood*

394 *Baltic* pattern on *Empress* shape. Handpainted flower design in two shades of blue on white earthenware. Made by Adams, now one of the Wedgwood group of companies. *Wedgwood*

395 Tableware made of china clay, ball clay, flint and hard purple stone. The shape was designed by David Queensberry MSIA HON DES RCA; and the pattern, which is an unusual combination of blue and green called *Spanish Garden*, was designed by Jessie Tait, one of Midwinter's resident designers. First produced 1966. Made by Midwinter Ltd of Burslem. *Council of Industrial Design*

Wedgwood remarked about this to Thomas Bentley in 1779–see page 96).

In the 1920's some art deco designs were about, with uncomfortable triangular teapots and cups; in the 1930's pastel colours took over with feeble little flowers, though plain colours were in greater demand than patterned ware. In the 1940's people were glad of anything that they could get, and most of them had to make do with plain white or 'export rejects' which often meant nineteenth century engraved designs printed in blue, pink or black (the old Willow pattern has never gone out of production). The 1950's produced some rather weak floral patterns in pale colours, both symmetrical and asymmetrical, on newly designed rimless or coupe-shape plates.

The 1960's show a return to the old traditional patterns, with a sprinkling of rather brighter coloured somewhat hectic designs, as well as some really interesting new work from some of the smaller potteries. In the kitchen-ware section, a good deal of re-thinking and re-designing has been done, with varying degrees of success. Some designs are extremely efficient, especially the ranges of ware intended for easy stacking. But for the most part oven-to-table ware designs have merely made 'polite' the old wholesome casserole, by altering its shape and adding a few flowers or stripes.

As it is extremely expensive to put a new design on the market, the manufacturers are naturally cautious. In the interests of economy, many firms are making all their ware in the same basic shapes, merely applying different surface designs. This means a simplification of production and much less storage space is needed for moulds.

The manufacturers are in somewhat of a dilemma. On the one hand, at the moment the main bulk of consumers are demanding traditional designs; on the other the manufacturers are being attacked for being unadventurous and die-hard. Some reputable, old-established firms have tried to put over what they thought were good modern designs, often with disastrous results, so they have cut their losses and have gone back to reproducing old designs, which they knew they could sell. Part of the trouble is that the manufacturers tend not to put full trust in their designers, whose designs are often mutilated by committee decisions. However some of today's firms have employed free-lance design consultants and have gone all out to introduce new patterns designed by the best contemporary designers, and have done very well. Some of the smaller firms, whose roots are not so firmly embedded in the past are breaking new ground in both design and techniques with considerable success. The Purbeck, Hornsea and Portmeirion potteries are all doing good, exciting and very individual work, using brilliantly coloured glazes and robust patterns especially appreciated by the younger generation.

It seems that it is the newer, smaller firms that are more willing to explore new fields, while the older firms are content to stick to what they know they can make and sell well, and who can blame them?

My only fear is that, with increasing technical advances, mechanization and the consequent loss of quality in the old sense of the word, the time may come when it will be necessary to re-think the whole situation before the old designs become such travesties of their former selves that nobody will want them.

396

397

396 *Chartreuse*. An old traditional Mason design, transfer printed in outline and hand painted in several greens, pale yellow and finished with touches of brightly burnished gold. Typical of the kind of designs the Mason factory was producing in the 1820's. The jug is exactly the same shape as were the earlier Mason jugs. It was known as the *Hydra* shape. Made by Mason's Patent Ironstone China Ltd. Jug 6″ high. *Mason's Ironstone China Limited*

397 *Napoleon Ivy*. A traditional Wedgwood design on Queensware. This was reputed to have been supplied to Napoleon during his exile on St Helena. The pattern first appeared in 1815 as a hand painted design in shades of green. The present version was first produced in 1906 in the form of a grey underglaze transfer print, filled in with rich dark green enamels. *Wedgwood*

398
399

214

400

398 *Windsor*. This design by Ridgways is a version of a blue transfer printed design called *Asiatic Pheasants*, that was very popular in the nineteenth century. This present day version has the original central design combined with a rather heavier and more ornate border. It is available today printed in either blue or red. The shape *Majestic*, is exactly the same as that used for the *Willow* and *Spring Garden*. *Allied English Potteries*

399 *Willow*. Booths' version of this blue transfer design, which has been available in many forms and made by innumerable potters, ever since John Turner of Caughley assisted by Thomas Minton engraved it in 1780. This version has a brightly burnished gold edging. Made by Booths, now a member of the Allied English Potteries group. *Allied English Potteries*

400 *Spring Garden*. A fairly new design produced by Ridgways based on a nineteenth century transfer printed pattern. The *Majestic* shape was first introduced in 1896. The colouring is an attractive mixture of soft greens and yellows. *Allied English Potteries*

401

402

401 Pint and half pint mugs made in hard-fired earthenware in two tones of brown. Designed by W. V. Cole and made at the Rye Pottery in 1969. *Council of Industrial Design*

402 Souvenir mug made of black and white jasper ware. Designed specially for Wedgwoods and for a souvenir competition organized by the Council of Industrial Design. Each letter incorporates a British sporting scene from Lords Cricket Ground to the Boat Race. Designed by Richard Guyatt. Height 4″.

403

404

405

403 Coffee ware in a Greek Key pattern designed by Susan Williams-Ellis for the Portmeirion Pottery. As well as black on white, this design is also made in black and turquoise and black and orange. Height of coffee pot 13".
The Portmeirion Pottery was started in 1962 by Susan Williams-Ellis and her husband, who bought up two potteries at Stoke-on-Trent: Gray's and Kirkhams. Kirkhams pottery made scientific and chemists' pottery and inspired by the simple geometric shapes which distinguish products in this line, Miss Williams-Ellis has produced a complete new range of shapes for kitchenware etc. Her work has both originality and great vitality.

404 Some pieces from the *Heirloom* range, designed by the design team and made at the Hornsea pottery in 1967. The range is produced in three colours, brown, blue and green. The Hornsea pottery began in a very small way just after the last war, it now employs nearly two hundred people and the output is somewhere about 70,000 pieces a week, many of which are exported all over the world. The designs are lively, the colours brilliant and the ware is very well made.

405 A cheese dish from the *Totem* range of designs by Susan Williams-Ellis for the Portmeirion Pottery of which she is Chairman. This design is made in amber, olive, cobalt and white glazes. Height 4¾".

217

406

406 Coffee cans made of fine quality earthenware, slip-decorated and hand turned. Called by the makers their *Channel Island* range. Top left: Guernsey: burnt orange. Alderney: French blue or green. Sark: blue, grey or honey and black. Jersey: French blue or green. Shape designed by Judith Onions DES RCA. Pattern Sark: Martin Hunt DES RCA. Jersey, Guernsey, Alderney: Judith Onions. First produced 1967 and made by T. G. Green Ltd of Church Gresley. *Council of Industrial Design*
These designs are in the tradition of Mocha ware, which used to be made by the same firm. See page 164.

407 Stoneware coffee set designed by Robert Jefferson DES RCA. Dark brown glaze with gold decoration. Made in 1968 by the Purbeck Pottery Ltd. The height of the coffee pot is $10\frac{1}{4}''$. The Purbeck Pottery was started in Bournemouth in January 1966 to produce stoneware tableware, using local clays from the Purbeck Hills. The ware is fired to 1250°, is completely vitrified and ovenproof. Normal factory methods are used for the making, decorative techniques rely on the texture and colour of the glazes and on silk screen printing. 85% of the production of this small but extremely go-ahead factory is exported.

408 The *Compact* range of earthenware by the Poole Pottery. This is a carefully thought out range of fifteen pieces designed by Robert Jefferson DES RCA in 1964, to be space and labour saving and versatile enough to fit into any setting. It is oven-proof, stackable and multi-purpose.

407

408

409
410

411

409 A range of stoneware containers for industrial purposes. There is something extremely
satisfying about these well-made absolutely simple basic shapes. *Royal Doulton Potteries*

410 Casseroles in the *Sterling* range, designed by Robert Minkin, DES RCA MSIA and made by
Wedgwood. It is decorated with a rich chestnut brown glaze. The largest casserole has a
capacity of 6 pints. *Wedgwood*

411 An oven-to-table ware range introduced in 1965, which has a chunky textured quality which is
achieved through a combination of moulded relief and new specially developed glazes. This
Pennine range is a rich brown colour with amber highlights. It was designed by Eric Owen
MSIA, Wedgwood's chief modeller, and of course made by Wedgwood. *Wedgwood*

Index